Alvar Aalto Houses
Timeless Expressions
アルヴァ・アアルトの住宅 ― その永遠なるもの

Alvar Aalto, photo by Antti Bengts

Architecture and Urbanism
June 1998 Extra Edition
Alvar Aalto Houses

建築と都市
1998年6月臨時増刊号
アルヴァ・アアルトの住宅

©1998 by A+U Publishing Co., Ltd.
Printed in Japan

Publisher/Editor:
Nobuyuki Yoshida
Editorial Associate:
Erwin J.S. Viray
Design Consultant:
Massimo Vignelli
Editorial Staff:
Mie Arioka
Natsuko R. Yamamoto

Published by A+U Publishing Co., Ltd.
30-8 Yushima 2-chome, Bunkyo-ku,
Tokyo 113-0034, Japan
Phone: (03)3816-2935
Fax: (03)3816-2937
E-mail: aandu@nisiq.net
URL: http://www.nisiq.net/~aandu

Distribution and order inquiries:
Japan Architect Co., Ltd.
31-2, Yushima 2-chome, Bunkyo-ku,
Tokyo 113-8501, Japan
Phone: (03)3816-2532
Fax: (03)3816-2937
Price Outside Japan:
¥5,000 + ¥1,500 (seamail postage)

© a+u 建築と都市
発行日：1998年6月1日
発行者／編集者：
吉田信之
エディトリアル・アソシエイト：
エルウィン・J・S・ビライ
デザイン・コンサルタント：
マッシモ・ヴィネリ
編集スタッフ：
有岡三恵
山本奈津子

定価：4,300円（本体4,095円）送料450円
振替：00130-5-98119
発行所：株式会社エー・アンド・ユー
〒113-0034東京都文京区湯島2-30-8
電話：(03)3816-2935
FAX：(03)3816-2937
E-mail：aandu@nisiq.net
URL：http://www.nisiq.net/~aandu
印刷：大日本印刷株式会社
大取次：トーハン・日販・大阪屋・中央
社・栗田出版・誠光堂
禁無断転載

Contents

4	Editor's Foreword
6	Essay: Markku Lahti *Alvar Aalto's One-family Houses:* *Paradises for Ordinary People*

1920-1940

24	House for Terho Manner
30	Villa Vekara
34	Aalto's Own House and Studio
44	Residence for Manager, Sunila Pulp Mill
52	House for Chief Engineer, Tampella Mill
60	Villa Mairea
81	Drawings of works in 1920-1940

1941-1960

102	House for Site Manager, Ahlström
108	Experimental House
122	Maison Carré
134	Manager's House B, Enso-Gutzeit
142	Manager's House C, Enso-Gutzeit
149	Drawings of works in 1941-1960

1961-

166	Maison Aho
174	Villa Oksala
180	Villa Kokkonen
188	Villa Skeppet
197	Drawings of works in 1961-
213	Essay: Matti Sanaksenaho *Visiting the Houses of Aalto*
225	Map
226	Chronology
230	Biography of Writers and Photographer
231	Credits and Acknowledgements

目次

表紙：ムーラッツァロの実験住宅
背表紙：ヴィラ・マイレア
写真：ヤリ・イエッツオネン

4 編集者序文

6 論文：
マルック・ラティ
アルヴァ・アアルトの住宅：普通の人々のためのパラダイス

1920-1940

24 マンネル邸
30 ヴェカラの夏の家
34 アアルト自邸とスタジオ
44 スニラ製紙工場管理者の家
52 タンペラ製紙工場主任技術者の家
60 ヴィラ・マイレア
81 1920～1940の作品の図面

1941-1960

102 アハルストリョム社管理者の家
108 ムーラッツァロの実験住宅
122 メゾン・カレ
134 エンソ・グートツァイト社管理者の家B棟
142 エンソ・グートツァイト社管理者の家C棟
149 1940～1960の作品の図面

1961-

166 アホ邸
174 オクサラ邸別荘
180 コッコネン邸
188 シルツ邸
197 1961～の作品の図面

213 論文：
マッティ・サナクセンアホ
アアルトの住宅を訪ねて

225 作品所在地の地図
226 年表
230 著者・写真家・翻訳者略歴
231 クレジット・謝辞

Cover: Experimental House
Back cover: Villa Mairea
Photos by Jari Jetsonen

Editor's Foreword
編集者序文

「建築は生物学上の自然を原形として捉えなければならない」

アルヴァ・アアルト

『白い机－モダンタイムス（鹿島出版会、田中雅美訳）』より

巨匠といわれる建築家は必ず独自の建築的思想と表現方法を持っている。アアルトもやはりその一人である。彼の時代には、コルビュジエ、ライトさらにはグロピウスなどバウハウスの建築家たちがいて、クラシシズムから国際様式・機能主義へと展開してきた。アアルトもその大きな潮流に巻き込まれつつも、フィンランド独自の文化のなかで、他の建築家たちとは異なる手法をやがて展開していくのである。それは、自然を愛するヒューマニストとして建築を見つめるアアルトの表現方法であった。

アアルトが生まれて今年で100年を迎える。アアルトを知らない世代の一人として、改めて彼の作品を見つめてみると、その建築思想や設計の手法が驚くほど現代的であり、人間的であり、エコロジカルであり、そして優しさに溢れていることを理解する。アアルトの建築は一人歩きすることなく、謙虚さを失うことなく、落ち着きとさりげなさを持ち、多くの人から愛されてきた。それは、建築の中心に人間を据え、自然と人間の調和を最も大切に考える彼の建築理念に起因する。そしてこの建築理念こそが、アアルトからの次世代へのメッセージではないだろうか。

時代の移り変わりほどに人間は変化できないものである。人間の感性に語りかける空間も、実はそれほど変わらないものであろう。「人間が中心であるべき建築」を唱えてきたアアルトの建築は、それゆえ時を越えて「永遠なるもの」と呼ぶことができる。

大きな社会構造の変化のなかで、今世紀の建築に偉大なる足跡を残したアアルトの作品を知ることで、我々は21世紀へ継承される建築の理念を掴み、また、可能性を探ることができるのではないだろうか。

本書ではアアルトの住宅作品の軌跡をたどる。年代順に紹介する15作品は、彼の建築が時代と共にどのように変化し、何が変わらなかったのかを明確に示してくれるだろう。

ヴィラ・マイレアをはじめ、いくつかの住宅は完成してから60年以上になるが、その年月を感じさせず、フィンランドの厳しい自然条件の中で、その土地や住み手を優しく包み込み、今も静かに佇んでいる。

写真はフィンランドの写真家ヤリ・イエッツオネン氏が3年以上の歳月をかけフィンランドの豊かな自然とアアルトの住宅を撮り下ろしたものである。図面もアアルト財団から貴重なオリジナル・ドローイングを複写させて頂いた。そして、アアルト美術館館長であるマルック・ラティ氏が「アアルトを知らない世代へ、時を越えたアアルトのメッセージを伝えたい」という願いを込めた書き下ろし論文を掲載する。

吉田信之

"Architecture must be modeled after the biological forms of nature."

– Alvar Aalto
Nykyaika, Alvar Aallon tutustuminen Funktionalismiin, Göran Shildt

The masters of architecture always have their own architectural philosophy and means of expression. Aalto was no exception.
The architects of his age included Le Corbusier, and Wright, as well as Gropius and the Bauhaus architects. It was a period of transition from Classicism to the International Style and Functionalism. Although Aalto was caught up in this great tide, he eventually developed his own unique methodology. It was the methodology of a humanist who loved nature.
This year marks the 100th anniversary of Aalto's birth. As a member of a generation that knows little about him, I was surprised when a renewed examination of his work revealed that his philosophy and methods of design are astonishingly contemporary. They are human, ecological, and filled with gentleness. Aalto's architecture never forgets its origins and never loses its modesty. It is quiet and casual, and has been loved by many. This is the result of his architectural principles, which place the human at the center of architecture and give the highest priority to harmony between man and nature. Perhaps it is these principles which are Aalto's true message to the next generation.
Times change but people have not changed that much. In fact, spaces which appeal to human sensibilities have probably not changed much either. Aalto's architecture placed the human at the very center, and for that reason it is timeless.
Amid great changes in the structure of society, Aalto left work that remains one of the monuments of this century's architecture. A more thorough acquaintance with his work should provide us with architectural principles to take into the next century, and with insight into new possibilities.
This issue is devoted to Aalto's houses. Fifteen works are introduced in chronological order, so we can see clearly what changed with the times and what remained constant.
Villa Mairea and some of the other residences in this issue were completed more than 60 years ago. But they hardly give the impression of the passage of years. In the severe climate of Finland, they gently envelop their sites and inhabitants, and still stand as peacefully as ever.
The photos are by the Finnish photographer Jari Jetsonen, who spent three years photographing Aalto's houses in their beautiful natural settings. The plans are copies of the invaluable originals, reproduced through the kindness of the Alvar Aalto Foundation. The essay "Alvar Aalto's One-family Houses: Paradises for Ordinary People" addressing a younger generation was written especially for this issue by Markku Lahti, Director of the Alvar Aalto Museum.

Nobuyuki Yoshida

Alvar Aalto's One-family Houses:
Paradises for Ordinary People
Markku Lahti

アルヴァ・アアルトの住宅：人々のためのパラダイス
マルック・ラティ
田中雅美訳

As a young architect in 1925, Alvar Aalto wrote, "The only real objective of architecture is: build naturally. Don't overdo it. Don't do anything without good reason. Everything superfluous turns ugly with time."[1] Aalto realized this requirement for naturalness in his own architecture in many ways, whether it was a matter of siting the building in the landscape, or of the organization of space. Especially in the Villa Mairea (1937–1939), Aalto's most important one-family house, there is an almost bravura elegance in all its effortlessness, all its ease and all its self-evident truth.

Alvar Aalto's career as an architect lasted for fifty years from 1921 to 1976. During that time he was able to design almost one hundred one-family houses, more than half of which were built. This aspect of Aalto's work, however, has received little attention. One reason perhaps for this is that he 'disparaged' the design of private houses, to some extent at least, and they were published rather rarely. "For myself I want to point out that I am not particularly interested in the design of private houses except where there is an opportunity for experiment, which who knows, may later on be of some use in creating large groups of buildings and the community. There was plenty of opportunity for this kind of experiment in my design for the Gullichsens' Mairea."[2] It may well be that this quotation from 1944 reflects more the prevailing wartime situation than Aalto's innermost ideas.

Aalto's one-family houses can be divided naturally into three groups. In the first group the clients were mostly private individuals who were friends or relations of Aalto's, or who had some natural contact with him through art or cultural life, for example. Aalto did not design one-off houses to order for complete strangers.

The second clear-cut group is formed by those one-family houses where the client was an industrial establishment or some other corporation. These dwellings, designed for directors, engineers, doctors and other officials usually formed part of a larger entity such as a factory or residential area where the basis for the design task was anonymous and to a certain extent controlled by the rest of the scheme. Paimio Sanatorium (1929–1933) and the residential areas of the Sunila pulp mill (1936–1954) and the Enso-Gutzeit factory, Summa (1958–1960), for instance, were just such places.

The third group, which as a whole has been studied very little, is made up of Aalto's standard houses and type-plans, the first of which he designed in 1925 and the last in the early 1950s. At least a couple of thousand of these wholly or partly factory-made one-family houses have been built in different parts of Finland, especially in residential areas for the wood-processing industry.

From the very beginning, Aalto's housing design was guided by an idealism, the aim of which was to achieve better housing conditions equally for everybody. There was a social reformer inside him who set out heavy responsibilities for architecture. Aalto said, "Architecture cannot save the world, but it can act as a good example."[3]

Giving a speech in Sweden in 1957, which was published under the name *The Architect's Idea of Paradise*, he crystallized his philosophy as follows: "There is an ulterior motive, too, in architecture, which is always peeping out from around the corner, the idea of creating paradise. It is the only purpose of our buildings. If we did not carry this idea with us the whole time all our buildings would be simpler, more trivial and life would become—well, would life amount to anything at all?

Every building, every work of architecture, is a symbol which has the aspiration to show us that we want to build a paradise on earth for ordinary mortals."[4]

Aalto realized his idea of paradise on many different levels. He did not just design ordinary houses, but he often called his designs *villa*, *casa*, *manorhouse*, or *maison*, thus giving them added psychological value. Although he listened to the wishes of his clients and carried them out, he took the view that people very rarely had the right idea of the space they needed. He stretched the Villa Skeppet (1969–1970) by a few metres, and when the Villa Kokkonen (1967–1969) was finished, the client was surprised to find there were an extra 70 square metres in it.

Colour too had its place in Aalto's ideas about architecture. In his opinion a small building like a one-family house, should be light in colour to accentuate its form. Correspondingly in large building masses, dark materials, such as red brick, should be used. With only a few exceptions Aalto's houses are indeed all light in colour: he wanted Maison Aho (1964–1965) to be light-coloured too, but the severe atmospheric conditions in Lapland prevented rendering and painting.

In 1922, Alvar Aalto wrote, "When we see how bygone ages have been able to be international and unprejudiced and at the same time true to themselves we can accept the influences of ancient Italy, Spain and the new America with our eyes open. Our forefathers will always be our preceptors."[5] Italy particularly formed a treasure trove for Aalto which he drew on throughout his life. His honeymoon in 1924 opened a door for him to a culture whose importance he never ceased to emphasize both in his architecture and in his life. In an interview in an Italian newspaper in 1954, he said, "In Italy what speaks to me is primitivism, a fundamental and surprising way of setting important forms for the human scale."[6]

Aalto's eclecticism was not, however, a superficial borrowing of forms and influences for their own sake, but he always gave new significance to his references in a new overall totality. In this way Aalto's architecture achieved historic depth in a manner which links it in with the long traditions of European architecture.

After his honeymoon in 1925, Aalto wrote an important essay entitled *From the Doorstep to the Living Room*,[7] in which he dealt particularly with the home and the relationship between inside space and outside space. He observed how "the helpless and imperfect show up almost without exception in the way in which the inner parts of buildings are aesthetically linked with the open air." This is due to the cold northern climate, as a result of which spaces were, in his opinion, cut off from each other in a disproportionately strict way. Between the home and its immediate surroundings there has to be a connection of "refined ceremony" from the street to the garden and from the garden to the interior spaces. According to Aalto, the garden belongs to the home just as much as any room. The home has to have two faces: one is a direct link aesthetically with the open air, "the other—the face of winter—shows up in the warmth-enhancing interior design of our innermost rooms."

In the same essay Aalto deals with the psychological function of the English hallway "as a comparison with the free open air, under the roof of the home." In his opinion it is related to the atrium court of the patrician Pompeian villa with the sky as its roof. From his writing, a picture can be conjured up of the inside of Casa Aalto (Väinölä 1925–1926), the house Aalto designed for his brother, where a washing line complete with washing runs across the hall. "Everyday banality as a key factor architecturally, a piece of a Neapolitan street in Finnish home furnishing."

Aalto concluded his writing by emphasizing the importance of the presence of the human factor in the home: "But if you want my blessing on your home, it must have one further characteristic: every little detail there must reveal you yourself, somewhere in the forms of your home a weakness has to be deliberately visible there, your own weakness. Very well, perhaps this belongs to an area which is outside the scope of the architect's powers, but no architectural creation is complete without this characteristic."

Around the turn of the century the housing problem had come to the fore as the most important challenge for society in Finland just as in other parts of Europe. The population was moving from the countryside to the towns to look for work. The old, traditional way of living in the countryside was a multi-purpose home, where the various elements of life and work were combined. At the turn of the century it was replaced by a more differentiated urban living model, in which children and parents, kitchen and other domestic work, the public and the private all had their own spaces. Only now did the dwelling become a home for urban workers.[8]

The concepts of 'the beauty of everyday life' and 'the beauty of the home', pleasantness and cosiness, were attached to this development. At the turn of the century the home was thought of 'as the garments of the family', and the great ideal was the one-family house. That ideal has remained in Finland right up to the present day.

Alvar Aalto's architecture at the beginning of the 1920s was bound in with his own time, with its values and ideals. The dominant style in Finland was Nordic Classicism, whose vocabulary and style Aalto had adopted as a student.

In its time Nordic Classicism was an almost unique phenomenon in Europe. On the one hand it was the successor to Art Nouveau: internal spatial arrangements followed the old pattern; the curving lines and forms of Art Nouveau were replaced by straight lines. On the other hand white purity and simple style were characteristic of Classicism which thus paved the way for Functionalism. The prevailing period of austerity, when economy, utility and simplicity were necessary virtues forced things in this direction, too. The external characteristics of the style included symmetry, Classical colonnades and decorative motifs.

Alvar Aalto's relationship with Art Nouveau has been researched very little. His only Art Nouveau design was his 1920 diploma work at Helsinki University of Technology, for Jyväskylä Town Hall.[9] On the other hand his design principles from the 1920s right through to the 1970s were based on a totality, an overall synthesis which took into account the smallest details and the various elements of interior design as an essential part of the architecture. In this respect the step from Art Nouveau to the Villa Mairea, for example, is not a great one. There are no direct references to be found in his later writings to the architecture of the turn of the century, unless his obituary for Eliel Saarinen, in which Aalto emphasized the significance of Finnish Art Nouveau as a synthesis of the national and the international, can be counted as such.[10]

Aalto's Classical period included almost 20 designs for single-family houses, most of which were in fact alterations and repairs to existing buildings. The Villa Karpio (1923) in Jyväskylä, for instance, was originally a chicken house, which Aalto turned into a small single-storey dwelling. The huge curved verandah and the house's stepped connection with the steep slope have been skilfully accomplished.

In the facade of the Terho Manner house (1923) there is an extravagance rare for Aalto. The Empire-style colonnade of the open verandah and the pediment which it carries seem to belong to another world as far as scale is concerned. Strict symmetry is emphasized by the wings on both sides of the main building containing spaces for farmwork and storage. The overall design is complemented by a well housing which Aalto designed as a miniature temple.

There is a firm grip, however, in the design of the internal spaces. As a contrast to the eight-sided hall, the size and arrangement of the other rooms varies and the doors, for instance, are not located in the middle of the walls in the usual Classical manner, but irregularly. The free floor plan is of clear Art Nouveau origin.

The Alatalo Manorhouse designed a year later (1924) is clearly a more controlled overall entity. The symmetrical, well-proportioned facade reflects the clear floor plan, the core of which is a hall running through the building with a closed-in entrance at one end and a glazed verandah opening onto the park at the other.

The most distinctive building of Aalto's Classical period is the Villa Flora (1926), which was probably designed by Aino Aalto. The villa was the Aaltos' summer house on Lake Alajärvi, in a small inland district to which Alvar's parents had moved from Jyväskylä in 1918. The Villa Flora is a low wooden building with a white stucco finish. The turf roof continues on the lakeside as a canopy as big as the house, supported by a colonnade. The building's small scale and size—to begin with there was only a kitchen, living room and one bedroom—are as from a Mediterranean shepherd's idyll.

Functionalism very quickly gained a foothold in Scandinavia and especially in Finland from the end of the 1920s onwards. There were several reasons for this. The step from Classicism's stripped-down vocabulary of form to the even stricter asceticism of Functionalism was a fairly small one. It was helped along by the economic depression, beginning in 1929, and all the social problems that came with it, which struck Finland a few years later than the rest of Europe.

The slogans of Functionalism, 'the avoidance of superimposed decoration' and 'form follows function', found favourable though serious ground in Finland. The profound wisdom of the writer of the second of these quotations, the American Louis Sullivan, has been applied only superficially. Functionalism soon became a way of organizing society and the way of life of the private individual. Its aim was to provide a good and healthy dwelling and milieu for all, independent of their social standing.

Functionalism aimed to reach its goal by emphasizing the importance of industrial housing production, because it was seen as the only way to build housing at a sufficiently low cost. The idea of the machine culture, where rational efficiency and speed were the most important values, was held to be the ideal. Beauty was equated with extreme usefulness. In the words of Le Corbusier: "We shall arrive at a machine house, a mass-produced house which is healthy (also morally) and beautiful like our tools." The young Finnish architect P. E. Blomstedt put it with a hint of satire in his comment: "This is the age of the machine culture: all we need to do now is to add electric lights, toilets and spiral staircases to our perspectives and we will be up-to-date again."[11]

The essence of Functionalism, however, was intelligent and rational thinking in an overwhelming respect for and belief in progress. In terms of design it started from zero and rejected history as useless ballast. Its foundations were Le Corbusier's Cartesian principles: analytical geometry, internationalism, timelessness and universal applicability, independence of time and place.

In Functionalism the drive towards practicality and simplicity was taken to the extreme. Although glass, concrete and steel were old materials they were given a new significance. White was the only acceptable colour for buildings, sometimes supplemented by grey or black. Shiny steel came into kitchens and polished tiles came to floor finishes. Flat roofs and strip windows where the visible characteristics of the exterior architecture.

Alvar Aalto's connections with Functionalism came about through Sweden. An important intermediary was his friend, the architect Sven Markelius, who arranged for Aalto to be one of the junior participants in the second CIAM (Congrès Internationaux d'Architecture Moderne) in Frankfurt in 1929. Also taking part in the Congress were Le Corbusier, Hannes Meyer and Walter Gropius. Aalto had already travelled to Europe the previous year and seen a number of key Functionalist buildings. Through CIAM, however, he came into personal contact with the key figures of Modernism and struck up lifelong friendships with László Moholy-Nagy, Fernand Léger and Sigfried Giedion. At the same time Aalto was designing Paimio Sanatorium (1929–1933), which became for him an international breakthrough, one of the most important buildings of heroic Functionalism. Generally speaking however, it could be said that orthodox Functionalism was rare in Finland. Functionalist adaptations were dependent on local conditions and noticeably more practical.

From the very beginning Aalto's relationship with Functionalism was double-edged. His progressive thinking and optimistic belief in progress drew him into taking part eagerly in debate and to adopting many new ideas in his architecture. Aalto's 'better world' was to be achieved through rational analysis, modern technology and the redistribution of society. Paimio Sanatorium, for example, can be considered as a paradigm of analytical architecture in which the practical problems are analysed and resolved right down to the smallest details and where the whole is formed from the sum of the parts.

In many of Aalto's writings touching on Rationalism and Functionalism he deals with living and the home. He sets great store by a happy everyday life without constraints and a healthy and modest way of living based on economy and reality as a contrast to affected superficiality and a longing for luxury.

Aalto's viewpoint comes out especially clearly in his 1930 article *Our Dwelling as a Problem*.[12] The basis of his analysis is the 'room', which he links with ancient palace architecture, which has nothing in common with the present day. "No family can live in one room nor even two, if they have children. But any family can live well in an equivalent area if that area is divided up for a family for the activities and the life of its members. The dwelling is an area which forms a sheltered space for eating, sleeping, working and playing. The biodynamic shapes of these activities have to form the basis for the internal division of the dwelling..."

In the same article Aalto wrote about adapting norms and scientific principles to studying residential architecture: "There is no sense in studying the question of how miserable are the conditions in which an individual can remain alive... What we have to consider today is the question of what requirements have to be set for the dwelling, its production, and its use when it has to fulfil all the requirements of good social conditions on a minimum income."

As these quotations show, Aalto took a serious attitude towards questions of housing design and tried to find ways of solving the problems. At the same time they reveal Aalto's own ideas as departing from Functionalism's general lines. To him it was not just a question of the rational and technical analysis and form of activities but equally the psychological and social functions they include. The seeds of doubt about Functionalism had already been aroused in him in 1927, when he wrote, "There is no point in inventing new forms unless there is some new content."[13] He continued in the same vein in 1935: "The separation of form and function unerringly leads to anti-humanism."[14] And again: "Objects which can justifiably be called rational, nevertheless frequently suffer from a noticeable deficiency in human qualities."[15] Aalto's criticism is especially directed towards the superficiality of Rationalism; it had not gone deep enough into the psychological and human layers. In Aalto's ideas about architecture, the social aspect particularly had aroused his critical faculties. He could not approve the strict rules of Functionalism, but rather in his opinion it was essential to strike a balance between individual and collective interests. He saw empirical study and experimentation as a means to this end, and this marked the whole of his later work as much in urban planning as in his few single-family houses. Aalto wrote in 1944, "Making architecture more human means better architecture, and this means a much wider Functionalism than merely a technical one. The goals can only be achieved using architectural methods—by producing and combining different technical elements so that they permit man the most harmonious life possible."[16] And again: "Architecture cannot be developed step by step, beginning with the technical realities and going on to human activity in other, more complex areas. Planning must proceed in all of these simultaneously."[17]

In his criticism of Functionalism, Aalto was not the only one who emphasized that architecture as an art form has a broader task than function. To many others as well, architecture was not just an exercise of style, but it included metaphoric and symbolic significance. Hugo Häring, for instance, stressed the special nature of each and every task which had to be taken into account before starting on the actual design work.[18]

*

Aalto's 'most functionalist' one-family houses are the Villa Tammekann in Tartu in Estonia (1932) and the chief physician's house at Paimio Sanatorium (1930–1933). In these, Aalto adapted the principles of Bauhaus design and style almost entirely as they were. The buildings are white stucco with flat roofs, roof terraces, metal handrails, door handles and window frames, and the massing, to a large extent, follows the appearance of Gropius' designs. In neither of them are there any Aalto-like softenings in the handling of materials and forms. The special feature of the Villa Tammekann is the living room fireplace, which in the plans is located opposite a strip window running the full length of the wall. Unfortunately this detail was never built.

1. *Casa Aalto (Väinölä), 1925-1926, project.*
2. *Villa Karpio, Jyväskylä, 1923. Photo by M. Kapanen.*

1. カーサ・アアルト(ヴァイノラ)、1925～1926、計画案。
2. ヴィラ・カルピオ、ユヴァスキュラ、1923。

3. *Alatalo Manorhouse, Tarvaala, Laukaa, 1924. Symmetrical facade.*
4. *Alatalo Manorhouse, interior.*
Photos by M. Kapanen.

3. アラタロ領主邸、ラウカー、タルヴァーラ、1924、左右対称のファサード。
4. アラタロ領主邸、内部。

Aino and Alvar Aalto had lived in a one-family house designed in the spirit of Art Nouveau by the architect Wivi Lönn in a garden suburb of Jyväskylä from 1924 to early 1927. For the next nine years they lived in blocks of flats in Turku (1927–1933) and Helsinki. In 1934 they acquired a site in the still almost untouched surroundings of a street named Riihitie, in Munkkiniemi, and began to design their own house which was completed in 1936.

The Riihitie house was designed both as a family home and as an office. It was Aalto's first building to be constructed in Helsinki and worked as a kind of visiting card or specimen for clients. The building's two functions show up clearly from outside. The slender mass of the office wing is lightly rendered and whitewashed brick, with the structure of the material showing through. There are still clear references to orthodox Functionalism, too, in the location of the windows. The cladding material of the residential part is slender, dark-stained, timber battens. Aalto has tried to relieve the verticality of the wall by random distribution of the joints in the battens, so that the overall effect is almost curtain-like. The building has a flat roof and a large south-facing terrace.

In many of his writings Aalto stressed the building's connection between inside and outside space. He sited the Riihitie house as close as possible to the street, to leave as much space as possible in the sunny, south-facing courtyard. Although the streetside elevation is fairly closed-off and severe, it is softened by climbing plants and a stone path leading to the main door. The door opens surprisingly on the 'wrong' side, so that the host has a slight psychological advantage over his guests. Stairs lead up from the small entrance hall to the family's private apartments. A view to the living room opens up straight ahead and through its windows to the internal courtyard beyond. At one end of the living room are the kitchen and dining room; at the other a couple of steps lead up to the office space which is separated by a sliding door. In the Riihitie house working and living are joined effortlessly to each other.

There are already signs of the 'new' Aalto in the Riihitie house, of the Romantic Functionalist as he is sometimes called. Manifestations of this are the use of wood as a cladding material, the stone paths and walls in the courtyard and the planting; open hearths inside built of brick and the overall cosiness and intimacy of the interior design. The house reflects the Aaltos' ideology on furniture design and interior decoration, which ARTEK was founded in 1935 to market.

Whereas the Riihitie house is a modest building for working and living designed by a 'poor' architect, the Villa Mairea (1937–1939) in Noormarkku is a luxurious residence. Aalto sometimes compared the Riihitie house with the old Finnish farmhouse, where simple materials and uncluttered rather rough working methods create a harmonic whole.

The Villa Mairea on the other hand is full of apparently conflicting forms, materials and techniques, metaphoric references to international Modernism as much as to vernacular building traditions, to simple Japanese purity and to French elegance. The well-known architectural historian William Curtis has written, "It is as if Aalto could not stop sticking in new ideas and devices."[19] Many have, in the same way as Curtis, longed for some organization in the Villa Mairea to hold everything together.

The building's astonishing power—or ambience—does however, in some magical way, keep a hold on the contrasts. Aalto wrote in the specification that the Villa Mairea "is aimed at avoiding artificial architectonic rhythms, but form in itself has not been avoided when it can be realized in harmony with the structure or when it has been possible through it to add the kind of materials and finishes that by their nature are sympathetic to people."[20] Even though it is a residence for business entertaining, the Villa Mairea is at the same time in a spontaneous way, intimate and cosy.

The Villa Mairea was for Alvar Aalto an *opus con amore*. He was given a completely free hand in the design by the clients, his friends Maire and Harry Gullichsen. He was even inspired to create something new and exceptionally there were no economic restraints. Aalto has indeed written about the Villa Mairea as a one-off architectural case, the results of which could subsequently be given over to the use of every citizen. The Villa Mairea is sited on the top of a hill in a pine forest. Approaching the building, the first glimpse of it through the trees gives the impression of a light-coloured Modernist building. From closer range the building's abundant details and their metaphorical references begin to work. Aalto has often stressed the importance of the link between inside and outside space, the intermediate stage that leads the visitor into the house. In the Villa Mairea the entrance canopy is supported by rather densely placed tree trunks still with the bark on, which darken the space even in daytime. Inside the house, the gaze almost immediately falls on a second 'forest', which lines the stairs to the upper floor. Next to it a light and spacious view opens out onto the inner garden, which also could be construed as a typical Finnish lakeside landscape in miniature complete with stone walls and lakeside sauna. The whole is complemented by a small man-made hill. As well as being for spending time in, the garden is also and especially for looking at.

The plan of the Villa Mairea has much in common with Aalto's own house: private apartments situated upstairs, work spaces and rooms for entertaining downstairs. Maire Gullichsen's painting studio is located upstairs, at the west end, and its rounded form has been clad with timber battens as at Riihitie. In many of the forms and details there is a soft and curving, sensual elegance. In several places there are skilfully handcrafted details alongside modern, industrially manufactured objects.

The Villa Mairea is one of Alvar Aalto's key works. It is like a play where the whole repertoire or dramatis personae of Aalto's architecture, from forms and materials to different techniques and subconscious fantasies, have their own roles to play. The tone is in turn rational, irrational, romantic, emotional, organic, whatever.

In the Villa Mairea, Alvar Aalto has been able to show in a unique way and on many different levels, the full range of his abilities as a house designer all at one go. But social housing production and community planning had gained an important place in his architectural work at the same time. Planning of huge factory areas extended in the 1930s from urban planning to housing for individual workers. He studied the problems of type-plan houses and the opportunities and requirements of standardization for the whole of the decade, especially while teaching at MIT in the United States in 1940.

On his return to Finland, Aalto came up against a very real housing problem, when half a million refugees who had lost their homes in the war had to be rehoused. So up-to-date and carefully researched were his solutions to the problem, that with hindsight one could even imagine that Aalto had sensed the coming war and its consequences.

Aalto's fundamental idea was flexible standardization and mass production. What he meant by this was that structural components were to be standardized, not houses.[21] In this way it would be possible to build flexible spaces that could be altered and made larger as had traditionally been done in Karelia for instance, where a house would grow around the basic roomspace according to the needs of the moment, one log frame at a time. Aalto's 1940s AA-house is an excellent example of this ideology: the same basic type could be varied in 69 different ways. Indeed the criterion of flexibility is one of the cornerstones of Aalto's architecture, whether it be a question of museums or of small houses.

A couple of thousand of Aalto's standard houses were built in factory housing areas in various parts of Finland. His principles of flexible standardization were not more widely used, however, because economic aspects favoured longer production runs and thus cheaper solutions.

The war years and the end of the 1940s were a time of austerity in Finland and architects had few design commissions. When at the end of the decade Alvar Aalto won the competitions for Helsinki University of Technology, Säynätsalo Town Hall and the University of Jyväskylä, a new upswing began in his career. Säynätsalo Town Hall (1949–1952) became his next masterwork on an international scale. Red brick, wood and copper were his main materials now and into his vocabulary of form came the antique and the Mediterranean architecture of the Middle Ages, which became an inexhaustible source for Aalto's own architecture.

Not counting the standardized houses, Aalto's next one-family house after the Villa Mairea was his own summer residence, the experimental house at Muuratsalo (1952–1954). Aalto's first wife Aino had died in 1949, and in 1952 he married Elsa (Elissa) Mäkiniemi, a young architect who had been involved in the design of Säynätsalo. The experimental house became their hideaway, a cottage in the wilderness which only a few had the opportunity of visiting.

To Aalto, Muuratsalo, an island to the south of Säynätsalo was already familiar country at the beginning of the century. When his family moved to Jyväskylä in 1903 Alvar came across a new inland landscape, dominated by mountains, forests and lakes. The summer villa culture and travelling by water already at that time had an important place in the hearts of the government officials and teachers in the town.

The experimental house is built on the flank of a magnificent rocky outcrop rising from the lake. The proportions of the building and the technical approach to the foundations have been carried out on the terms of the surrounding nature. The brick part, built in the first stage, is finished outside in white rough-cast. Later on, the white-painted timber guest wing was built on the slope of the forest. The building has a heroic location resembling a Greek temple in its relationship with nature, but set against the green of the Finnish forest.

The warmth of the red brick in the central courtyard is a contrast to the white exterior. Aalto has divided the wall surfaces of the courtyard into fifty panels where he has tried out the durability and visual effect of different types of brick and methods of bricklaying. The rectangular courtyard paved with different panels of brickwork is dominated by an open fireplace in its centre, and green moss and white clover grow in the joints between the bricks.

The rooms of the main building are grouped in two wings around the central courtyard. In the northern part there is a combined living room and study, complemented by Aalto's gallery painting studio, and in the east wing there are bedrooms. The kitchen and sanitary facilities are located at the junction between the two, along with an ingeniously designed corridor leading to the guest wing.

The experimental house is not an easy building to approach, not only physically but also in terms of interpretation. Many of the basic elements of Aalto's architecture are to be found there. The central courtyard is perhaps the best example of the refined and sensitive manner in which Aalto so often broke down the boundary between inside space and outside space. From the living room there is a view over the courtyard to the lake, and from the bedroom window the tower of Muurame church (Alvar Aalto 1926–1929) can be made out through an opening in the west wall across the yard. From the kitchen a view opens up through two windows and across the corridor to the northern slope, by which guests usually approach the house.

There is a clear romantic and archaic spirit in the experimental house. The solitary walls and empty openings refer to something that had existed and been destroyed; they refer to the nostalgia of ruins. The building's historical dimension is not a superficial quotation however, but rather bound to and concealed within a subconscious frame of reference. William Curtis has used the phrase "hidden presences."[22]

The Villa Mairea and the Muuratsalo experimental house are linked by experiment and 'play', in its serious and positive sense. Both have a powerful, individual identity behind which there is a kind of family resemblance. Aalto's buildings are indeed impossible to place within strictly limited stylistic concepts or any other previously defined framework.

Maison Carré (1956–1961) at Bazoches-sur-Guyonne, fifty kilometres from Paris, is also a rather subjective building. Its genesis provides explanations for many of its architectural devices. The Parisian art-dealer Louis Carré had asked a Swedish friend whether he knew of a good architect who could design him a house. Carré became aware of Aalto's name in this way and after an exchange of letters the gentlemen agreed to meet in Venice in the summer of 1956, when the pavilion Aalto designed for the Biennale was opened. They struck up a life-long friendship at their first meeting. Carré and Aalto enjoyed each other's company enormously; they both loved red wine, and international art and cultural circles were part of everyday life for both of them.

Maison Carré is a residence which, in the same way as the Villa Mairea, combines work and private life. Aalto once again had a free hand to realise his ideas without any economic constraints. The floor plan of the building is apparently clear and cellular, and the rooms fulfilling various functions are grouped around an entrance hall located in the middle. The free-form wooden ceiling of the high hall is a memento of Viipuri Library. Into this space which is almost sacred in spirit, daylight enters rather thinly from side windows above the main door. The wall surfaces of the hall are lined with works of art and there are a couple of sculptures standing on the floor.

From the entrance hall wide steps lead down to the living room. From the windows running the full-length of the wall there are extensive views over the grassed garden area which is bordered by what is now a fairly dense forest. Once again Aalto skillfully leads visitors from the shadow to the light, from the upper level to the lower following the natural slope of the ridge. The 'public' spaces of the house also include a study/library beside the living room and a dining room tucked away peacefully behind the entrance hall.

The private rooms and the guest room are located on the south side of the house, where they have direct contact with nature. The ways into them are cleverly concealed behind an 'artwork wall' that divides the entrance hall. Aalto used the same theme later in the Maison Aho in Rovaniemi. The servants' quarters are upstairs.

Maison Carré is a white-rendered brick building whose elevation from the north is dominated by a low-pitched roof sloping in two directions in which distant abstract references to Frank Lloyd Wright's prairie houses can be seen or to Aalto's few one-family houses from the 1940s. The recessed entrance is located below the intersection of the roofs. The natural stonework is in the local sandstone. The south elevation is more sculptural and there are references in its proportions to the Muuratsalo experimental house, for instance.

Maison Carré is an 'Aaltoesque' complete work of art. Many of the small details and most of the furniture and light fittings of the 'public' spaces were carefully designed specifically for this house. Elissa Aalto's hand can be seen in several places. Once again the garden area is as a continuation of the inside space, the terraced slopes creating a gradual transition to the swimming pool sited lower down and from there onwards to the natural spaces of the forest. In the early years there was even a small vineyard starting straight from the wall of the house.

During the 1960s Aalto's architecture took a turn towards a more sculptural and monumental vocabulary of form. Sometimes in his later work there are references to eclectic and even Baroque characteristics. In his rare private houses, however, Aalto has preserved the personal touch. He designed only for friends whose personality and work have given their clear stamp to the houses.

Aalto designed the Villa Kokkonen (1967–1969) for his composer friend and academician colleague Joonas Kokkonen. The starting point for the design was the composer's most important tool, the grand piano, which set certain conditions for the other rooms. The studio is indeed separated from the other rooms by a lead-lined sliding door and its acoustics have been taken particularly into account. The studio rises above the rest of the building mass. Wall surfaces and the greater part of the floors and the structure are of wood, the external walls being battened in the same way as Aalto's own house at Riihitie.

There is an unusual degree of warmth and tranquillity. The building is hidden away among the trees and there is no clear facade. A covered way leads down from the main building to the sauna. Without thinking an old Finnish forest camp comes to mind, one which you notice only when you stumble across it. The character of the house is revealed inside: it is like a sensitive musical box in which every part has its place. Aalto has achieved the same kind of feeling in the living room of the Summa factory manager's residence.

The openly proud existence of the Villa Skeppet (1969–1970) is a contrast to the introverted expression of the Villa Kokkonen. The house was designed for Aalto's close friend and biographer Göran Schildt. Aalto wanted to build a house that would keep him in Finland!

In the Villa Skeppet, Aalto raised the living room above the garage making it higher than the rest of the building mass and emphasizing the special character of the space. There are

points in common with the massing of the Villa Mairea or the Riihitie house. Metaphorically, references to the writer's life at sea can also be discerned; in fact it is like the bridge of a ship from which a view opens up over the sea. The intimate inner courtyard behind the house with its free-form lily-pool is bounded on the other side by a small guest wing.
Despite the apparently stiff floor-plan there is an Aaltoesque elegance about the Villa Skeppet. The polymorphic space flows easily from the small, dimly-lit entrance hall, up two flights of steps to the well-lit living room. The dining area is located separately beside the kitchen in a similar way to the Muuratsalo experimental house, the Tiilimäki studio house or the Villa Oksala.

Aalto's internal architecture is marked by a distinct separation between 'public' and private. His living rooms are frequently reception spaces for business entertaining, which are carefully designed right down to the furniture. The place where the family assembles on a more everyday basis is often the dining area close to the kitchen. In all of Aalto's one-family houses there is at least one open fireplace which has an important role in the composition of the internal spaces. Sometimes they are simple and stripped down as at Riihitie and Muuratsalo, but more often they are like sculptures of great plasticity, positioned at points of climax within the spaces.
One-family houses form a varied and fascinating whole in Aalto's extensive output. In them the basic outlines of his architecture can be seen and the changes it underwent from the 1920s to the 1970s, but at the same time there is almost always a personal touch in them. The small buildings are firmly tied in with their surroundings which the architect has often shaped in the direction he desired by creating continuations of the inside spaces outside, intermediate spaces of some kind or the other. Often he has also closed off and sheltered an intimate inner courtyard by grouping the sauna and other outbuildings around it in the old vernacular manner.

The ideas of the 'small man' and nature recur in Aalto's architectural writings over and over again. Where he is concerned one could talk about ecological architecture long before the idea of ecology appeared. In 1940 Aalto wrote, "The architect's world concentrates on creating harmony, on tying together threads from the living future to the living past. The basis of it is man—with all his countless emotional threads—and nature, man included."[23]

(Translated from Finnish by Nicholas Mayow)

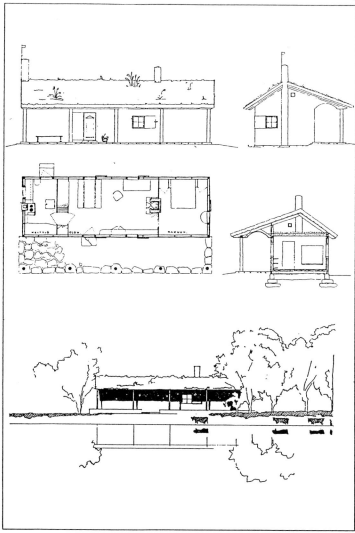

5. *Villa Flora, Aalto's summer house, near Alajärvi, 1926. Photo by M. Kapanen.*
6. *Villa Flora, drawings.*

5. ヴィラ・フローラ、アアルトの夏の家、アラヤルヴィ近郊、1926。
6. ヴィラ・フローラ、図面。

7. *Alvar Aalto, 1928. Photo by Turun Sanomat.*
7. アルヴァ・アアルト、1928。

1925年に青年建築家アルヴァ・アアルトは書いている。「建築における唯一の正しいねらいは『自然に無理なく建てる』ということである。誇張してはいけない。不必要なものをつくってはいけない。余分なものはすべて、時間の経過とともに見苦しくなる」[1]と。彼は自らの建築の中で、風景への建物の配置とか、建物内部の空間配列など、あらゆるかたちでこの自然というものを具現してみせた。特に、有名な個人住宅ヴィラ・マイレア（1937〜1939年）は、そのさりげなさ、落ち着き、明瞭さにおいて、ほとんど華麗までに優雅である。

アルヴァ・アアルトは、1921年から1976年まで50年以上にわたって建築家として活動した。その間、およそ100件に及ぶ一世帯住宅を設計し、半分以上を実現させた。ところが彼の作品の中でも、個人住宅はほとんど注目されていない。彼自身、それらを多少なりとも軽視していたことと、誌面に発表される機会がめったになかったことが一つの原因だろう。

「私の側から言わせてもらえば、後に大規模な建物群や共同体をつくるときのために役立つような実験を行えない限り、個人住宅の設計にそれほど興味を持っていないということです。その点、グリクセン家のヴィラ・マイレアを設計したときには、大いに実験のチャンスを与えてもらいました」[2]

1944年のこの言葉は、彼の本心を表す以上に、戦時中の状況をよく反映している。

アアルトの一世帯住宅は三つのグループに分けられる。一つめは、依頼主がたいてい親類や友人あるいは芸術や文化を通じてなんらかのつきあいのある人物の場合だ。まったく知らない人に個人住宅を設計することはなかった。

明確に類別できる二つめのグループは、企業やその他の共同体から依頼された一世帯住宅だ。工場長や技師、医師、公務員用に設計したこれらの住宅は、通常、工業地区や住宅地区全体の中の一部であるため、特色のない、ある程度既定された設計になる。パイミオ・サナトリウム（1929〜1933年）、スニラのアハルストリョム社の工場（1936〜1954年）、スンマのエンソ・グートツァイト社の工場（1958〜1960年）などの住宅地区がこれに該当する。

三つめは、1925年から1950年代初期にかけて設計した規格住宅とタイプ住宅の一群だが、ほとんど研究されていない。それらは一部または全体が工場生産された一世帯住宅で、特に木材加工工場の住宅地区など、フィンランドのいたるところに少なくとも2000戸以上建てられている。

当初からアアルトの住宅設計を方向づけていたのは、理想主義だ。より良い住環境をすべての人々に平等に与えるというのが、その目標である。彼は建築に重要な責務を課す社会改革者的な一面を持っていた。「建築が世界を救うことはできない。だが、最良の手本を示すことはできる」[3]と彼は言う。

1957年にスウェーデンで行なった「建築家のパラダイス考」と題する講演で、己の哲学を次のように明快に述べている。

「建築には、人目につかない片隅でチラチラと顔をのぞかせる隠れた思想、パラダイスをつくろうという思想があります。それこそ私たちの建物がめざす唯一の目標なのです。私たちが常にこの思想とともに歩まなければ、建物はどれもこれもさらに単純でつまらないものになってしまうでしょうし、生活も——大体からして、そんなものが生活と言えるでしょうか。どの建物にも、建築芸術を象徴するどの作品にも、人々のために地上にパラダイスをつくろうとしていることを伝えたいという願いが込められています」[4]

彼はパラダイス考をあらゆる面で実践した。ごくありふれた住宅を設計するつもりはなく、作品をよくヴィラとかカーサ、領主邸、メゾンなどと呼び、心理的な付加価値を与えた。彼は確かに施主の希望を聞いてそれを実行したけれども、一方で、人々が必要な空間を正しく把握していることはめったにないと考えてもいた。たとえばシルツ邸（1969〜1970年）は、予定よりも数メートル余分に拡大したし、コッコネン邸（1967〜1969年）が完成したときには、70㎡もの空間が追加されているのを見た施主を驚かせたものだ。

アアルトの建築観の中では、色彩もまた重要な位置を占めている。たとえば一戸建住宅などの小さな建物は、形を強調するためにも薄い色合いにするべきで、逆に大きな建物では、赤レンガのような濃い色を使う方がよいというのが彼の意見である。数件の例外を除けば、彼の住宅はほとんど色彩が薄い。アホ邸（1964〜1965年）も薄くしたかったのであろうが、ラップランドの厳しい気候条件がスタッコや塗料を塗るのを阻んだ。

1922年にアアルトは書いている。

「過去の時代がいかに国際的で偏見がなく、同時に自身に忠実であり得たのかを見てみれば、古代イタリアやスペイン、現在のアメリカから私たちは目を見張るばかりの刺激を得ることができるだろう。祖先は今なお、私たちの偉大なる師である」[5]

特にイタリアは、彼にとって宝の詰まった引出しのようなもので、生涯、ときどき開けては覗いた。1924年のイタリアへの新婚旅行が文化への扉を開いてくれてからというもの、建築においても生活においても、この文化の意義を力説し続けた。1954年にインタヴューされたイタリアの新聞記事で、「原始主義と、人間のスケールに適した大事な形態を決定する基本的かつ意外な方法を、イタリアは私に語りかけてくれます」[6]と言っている。

けれどもアアルトの折衷主義は、形態と効果を皮相的に借用するのではなく、新しい全体像の中で借用部分に常に新しい意義を与えた。このようにアアルトの建築はヨーロッパ建築の古い伝統に結びつくことによって、歴史的な奥深さを備えた。

1925年の新婚旅行の後、『ドア・ステップからリヴィング・ルームへ』[7]という注目すべきエッセイを書き、特に住宅及び内部の居住空間と屋外空間の関係に触れている。「建物内部を戸外へ美的につなぐという重要なポイント地点である玄関は、ほとんど例外なく何か救いようのない不調和を感じさせる状態だ」と述べている。これは、暖かい屋内と寒い屋外の区切りを余儀なくさせる、北欧の寒冷な気候に起因している。しかし区切りがあまりにも厳重すぎて、均衡がとれていないと彼は感じたのだ。家と隣接地の間には、通りから庭へ、庭から屋内へと移行する「優雅な儀式」とでもいえる関係がなければならない。庭は、他の部屋と同じぐらい家に属するものだ、というのがアアルトの考え方だ。家は二つの顔を持たなければならない。一つは美しい形で戸外へ直結する顔、「もう一つは奥の部屋の温度を高めるインテリア・デザインに見られる『冬の顔』」である。

同じエッセイの中で、「屋根の下に持ち込まれた開放的な外界の象徴」としてのイングリッシュ・ホールの心理的役割にも触れている。空を屋根代わりにしているポンペイの貴族邸の中庭とイングリッシュ・ホールは、かなり遠い親戚関係にあるという意見だ。文を分かりやすくするために添えたカーサ・アアルト（弟ヴァイノのために設計した「ヴァイノラ」1925〜1926年）の室内図では、吹抜け天井を持つホールの上階に、洗濯物を干したロープが張られている。

「日常生活の気どりのなさを建築の主要素にし、ナポリの路地を思わせる光景をフィンランドの住宅のインテリアに採り入れた」

家の中で人間の存在を表す要素が大切であることを強調しながら、以下のように文章を締めくくられている。「しかし、もし読者諸氏が自分の家のために私のアドヴァイスを得たいと思われるなら、さらにもう一つの特色を家に与えなさいと私は言おう。どこか小さなディテールの中で、あなた自身をさらけ出しなさい。家の形態のどこかに故意に弱点を、そう、あなたの弱点を見せるのです。これは建築家の権威が届かない範疇に属することだが、この特色なしには、どのような建築の創造も完全ではない」と。

19世紀末から20世紀初頭にかけて、他のヨーロッパ諸国と同様、フィンランドでも社会が抱える大きな課題として、住宅問題が浮上した。人々が仕事を求め

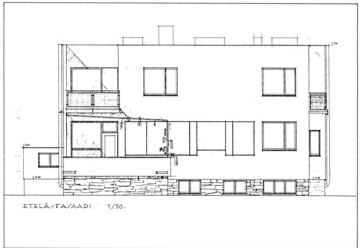

8. Villa Tammekann, Tartu, Estonia, 1932. Photo by Markku Lahti.
9. Villa Tammekann, south elevation.

8. ヴィラ・タンメカン、エストニア、タルトゥ、1932年。
9. ヴィラ・タンメカン、南立面図。

て地方から都市へ流入したのだ。田舎地方での昔からの伝統的な居住形態とは、仕事と生活のあらゆる要素が一つにまとまった多機能な住宅だった。当時、それにとって代わったのが、子供と両親、台所仕事とその他の家事、パブリックとプライヴェートなど、それぞれの専用空間を備えた、ますます分化が進む都市型居住形態だ。そしてやっと今、単に住むだけの場所が、都市労働者のための住宅になったのだ。[8]

この発達に、さらに「日常生活の美」と「住宅の美」、快適さとくつろぎやすさを組み入れるようになった。20世紀初頭、家は「家族を装う衣裳」であると考えられ、最高の理想が一戸建住宅だった。フィンランドでは、この理想が今日でもそのまま残っている。

1920年代初期のアルヴァ・アアルトの建築は、その時代の理想と価値観に結びついている。フィンランドで勢力があった様式は北欧古典主義で、学生時代のアアルトは、その表現法とスタイルを採り入れていた。

北欧古典主義というのは、当時のヨーロッパではきわめて特異な現象だった。一方ではアール・ヌーヴォーを後継していて、内部空間は従来の方法に従った構成になっている。ただ、アール・ヌーヴォーの丸をおびた線と形はまっすぐに変えられている。また一方で、古典主義の特徴である白の清潔さとシンプルなスタイルが、機能主義への道を拓いてくれた。さらにこのように方向づけた一因は、世の中をおおっていた経済の低迷で、必然的に節約と実用性と簡素さが美徳とされた。外観の特徴は、シンメトリーとクラシカルな柱廊と装飾モティーフなどである。

アルヴァ・アアルトとアール・ヌーヴォーの関係は、ほとんど研究されていない。1920年にヘルシンキ工科大学で課題としてつくったユヴァスキュラ市庁舎[9]が、彼の唯一のアール・ヌーヴォー・スタイルの設計だ。いっぽう、1920年代から1970年代に至るまで、彼の設計方針は常に全体性と統合を基本にし、建築に欠くことのできない一部分として、小さなディテールや内装の様々な要素にも留意してきた。その意味では、アール・ヌーヴォーから、たとえばヴィラ・マイレアまでの道のりはさほど長くなかった。故エリエル・サーリネンへの追悼文の中で、国内および国際的な統合としてのフィンランドのアール・ヌーヴォーの意義を力説しているが、それを除けば、後の彼の論文や記事には今世紀初頭の建築に直接言及した文章は見られない。[10]

古典主義の頃のアアルトは、およそ20件ほどの一戸建住宅を設計しているが、その大部分は現存の建物の改築や改修作業だった。たとえばユヴァスキュラのヴィラ・カルピオ（1923年）は、もともと鶏舎だった建物を小さな平屋住宅に改造したものだ。アーチをモティーフにした広いヴェランダと、急勾配の敷地に合わせて段状にした建物の配置がみごとである。

アアルトにしては珍しい豪壮さがテルホ・マンネル邸（1923年）のファサードに見られる。ポーチに建つ帝国様式の列柱やその上のペディメントは、スケールの面からいっても彼とは異質の世界のもののように感じられる。母屋の両側に広がる翼（ウィング）が厳密なシンメトリーを強調していて、そこには農作業用の空間や物置が収められている。構成全体の仕上げとして、神殿の形をした小さな東屋を加えた。

内部空間はもう少し自由に設計されている。八角形のホールに対比させるように、他の各部屋の大きさや配列を多様にし、特にドアは、壁の中央に設置するという古典主義の定石を踏まず、変則的にした。1階平面図は、明らかにアール・ヌーヴォーを原点にしている。

1年後に設計したアラタロ領主邸（1924年）は、全体がもっと厳格に統制されている。均整のとれたシンメトリーのファサードは、建物を貫くホールを核とする明快な平面プランを反映している。建物前面に閉ざされたポーチがあり、反対側には庭に向いたガラス窓を持つヴェランダがある。

古典主義の頃の特徴が最もよく表れている住宅が、ヴィラ・フローラ（1926年）だ。これはおそらくアイノ・アアルトが設計したと思われる。1918年に両親が

ユヴァスキュラから引越した内陸の小さな村、アラヤルヴィに建てたアアルト家のサマー・コテージである。白いスタッコで仕上げた低い木造住宅だ。湖側の列柱まで芝屋根が庇のように延びている。建物は小さくて——当初は台所と居間と寝室一部屋しかなかった——地中海地方の牧歌的風景のようだ。

*

機能主義は北欧で、特にフィンランドでは1920年代末にあっという間に足場を築いた。これにはいくつかの理由がある。まず、古典主義の限定された形態言語から機能主義のもっとも厳しい制約までの行程は、決して長くなかった。さらに1929年に始まった経済不況と、それによって生じた社会問題が、機能主義の発展を促した。フィンランドがそのような社会問題に突き当たったのは、他のヨーロッパ諸国よりも数年遅れてからだった。

「装飾の追放」「形は機能に従う」という機能主義のスローガンは、折りよく本格的にフィンランドに根をおろした。二つめのスローガンの作者、アメリカ人のルイス・サリヴァンの奥深い名言から、ほんのうわべだけが借用された。やがて機能主義は、社会と個人の生活を組織化する手段となってゆく。社会的地位に関係なく、すべての人々に快適で衛生的な住居と住環境を提供するというのが、そのねらいだった。

機能主義は、住宅を工場生産する意義を強調することによって、目標を達成しようとした。それが、納得のいく安さで住宅を建てる唯一の方法だと考えられたからだ。そうして合理的な効率とスピードを最も高く評価する機械文化が、理想としてかかげられた。美しさも最高に有益であるとされた。「私たちは機械住宅にたどり着くでしょう。道具と同じように衛生的で（品格も備えた）美しい大量生産の住宅です」とは、ル・コルビュジエの言だ。フィンランドの若い建築家P・E・ブロムステッドは、1928年に多少の皮肉を含んだコメントを述べている。「機械文化の時代がやってきました。私たちが今為すべきことは、電光とトイレットと螺旋階段をパースペクティヴに付け加えることです。そうすれば、再び時代の先端をいけるでしょう」[11]

しかしながら機能主義の真髄は、進歩に対して絶対的な敬意と信仰を持ったうえでの、聡明で合理的な考え方だった。デザインの面でいうと、機能主義はゼロからスタートし、歴史を無用な足枷であるとして拒絶した。土台となったのは、ル・コルビュジエが唱えた、解析幾何学、国際性、時代の超越、普遍性、時代や場所に左右されない、というデカルトの原理である。

機能性と簡素さの追求は極度に達した。ガラス、コンクリート、スティールなどの従来の材料に、新しい役割が与えられた。建物の色合いとしては、白が唯一好ましい色とされ、時には白を補うために黒や灰色を加えた。光沢のあるスティールが台所に、硬質タイルが床面の仕上げに使われた。そして陸屋根と水平連続窓が、建物外観の目立った特徴だった。

アルヴァ・アアルトは、スウェーデンを通じて機能主義に関わるようになった。重要な橋渡しをしてくれたのは、友人のスウェーデン人建築家スヴェン・マルケリウスだ。1929年にフランクフルトで開かれたＣＩＡＭ（Congrés Internationaux d'Architecture Moderne、近代建築国際会議）第二回大会にアアルトが参加できるように手配してくれたのが、他でもないマルケリウスだったのだ。ル・コルビュジエ、ハンネス・マイヤー、ワルター・グロピウス等の面々もこの会議に出席していた。前の年にアアルトはヨーロッパを旅行し、機能主義の主要な建物をすでに数多く見ていた。とはいえＣＩＡＭを通じて、ラズロ・モホリ＝ナギやフェルナン・レジェ、ジークフリート・ギーディオン等、モダニズムの中心人物と個人的に親しくなり、終生の友情を結べたのは有意義だった。

この当時に設計したパイミオ・サナトリウム（1929〜1933年）は、国際的な躍進を遂げるきっかけをつくり、大胆な機能主義の代表的建築の一つになった。しかし概していえば、フィンランドには正統な機能主義というのはほとんどなかったといえるだろう。機能主義を取り入れるときに、土地の条件に左右されたし、実用性の方がずっと重視されたからだ。

アルヴァ・アアルトの機能主義との関係は、最初から二分化していた。発展に対して前向きの姿勢と楽天的な信念を持つ彼は、熱心に討論に加わり、多くの新しいアイディアを己の建築に採り入れた。アアルトが言う「より良い世界」は、合理的な分析と近代科学技術と新分類法を通して達成されようとしていた。たとえば、パイミオ・サナトリウムは、実際問題を小さなディテールに至るまで分類、解決し、そんな各部を集めて全体を形づくるといった分析的建築の範例として考察できる。

合理主義と機能主義に関する多くの著述の中で、アアルトは居住と家について論じている。見せかけだけの皮相性や贅沢への憧れに対比させて、束縛のない楽しい日常生活や、家計の実状にあわせた健康で質実な暮らし方を称賛している。

1930年に書いた「問題としての住居」[12]と題する記事に、彼の考え方がとりわけ明快に表れている。分析の出発点は「部屋」で、彼はそれを現代とはまったく共通点のない古代の宮殿に結びつけて考えている。

「どんな家族ももし子供がいれば、一部屋では、いや二部屋であろうと、生活することはできない。ところが同じ面積でも、家族の各人の行動や生活にあわせて空間を分割すれば、どんな家族でも快適に暮らすことができる。住宅とは、食事、睡眠、仕事、遊びのための保護空間を構成する場所である。このような生物力学上の行動形態が、住宅内部を分割するときの基本となるべきで……」

同じ記事の中で、住宅建築の研究に機能主義の規準と科学の原理を応用することについて書いている。「人はどの程度ひどい環境の中で生きられるかといった問題を研究しても、何の意味もない。現在、私たちが考えなければならないのは、最低限の収入で住宅が好ましい社会環境の必要条件を満たさなければならない場合、住宅およびその生産と使用に何を課すべきかということだ」

彼が住宅設計の問題に真剣に取り組み、解決の道を探ろうとしていたことを、上記の引用文は示している。同時に機能主義の一般路線から外れた彼の考え方も思わず表れ出ている。彼にとっての機能主義は、単に合理的、技術的な分析や活動形態ではなく、心理的、社会的役割が同じくらい含まれていた。「新しい内容が伴わないのなら、新しい形態を創作しても意味がない」[13]と書いた1927年頃には、すでに機能主義に対する疑問が芽生えていたのだ。その延長上で、1935年には「形態と機能の分離は、間違いなく非人間性に行き着く」[14]と言い、さらに「当り前のように合理的と呼ばれるものは、えてして人間的な要素が著しく欠如しているという欠点がある」[15]と付け加えた。アアルトの批判の矛先は、とりわけ合理主義の皮相性に向けられた。合理主義は、心理的、人間的な面の深層にまで充分に掘り下げられていないからだった。

アアルトの建築観を見ると、特に社会的見地に立ったときに、批判精神が呼び起こされるようだ。機能主義の厳しい規定を是認できなかった彼は、個人と集団の利害のあいだに調和を見いだすことこそが、本質的な問題だと捉えていた。そしてその問題に取り組むには、経験にもとづく研究と実験が必要であると考えた。何件かの一戸建住宅や都市計画など、彼の後の作品にはすべて、この考え方が明確に表れている。1944年に次のように書いている。

「建築を人間的にするというのは、よりよい建築をつくることを意味し、単に技術上だけではないもっと広義の機能主義を意味している。人間が最も調和のとれた生活を送れるようにするために、様々な技術部品をつくりだし結合させるといった建築的手法によってのみ、その目標を達成できる」[16] さらにこう続ける。「建築というのは、技術面から始まって、その後、もっと複雑な領域の人間の活動面へ移るといったように、段階的に進展するものではない。設計するときに、これらすべての領域を同時に処理しなければならないのだ」[17]

機能主義の批評の中で、芸術形態としての建築には機能よりももっと広範な課題があると力説したのは、アアルトだけではない。他の多くの人にとっても、建築は様式の単なる練習ではなく、隠喩的、象徴的な意味を含んでいた。たとえばフーゴ・ヘーリングは、実際の設計を始める前に留意すべきそれぞれの課

題の特性を強調した。[18]

*

アアルトの「最も機能主義色が強い」一戸建住宅には、エストニアのタルトゥに建つヴィラ・タンメカン（1932年）と、パイミオ・サナトリウムの医長の住宅（1930〜1933年）がある。これらの建物では、バウハウスの設計及び様式の基本方針を、ほとんどどそのまま適用した。白漆喰、陸屋根、ルーフ・テラス、金属製の手摺とドアの取っ手と窓枠、マッスなど、どれもこれもグロピウスが設計した建物の外観に倣っている。材料と形を扱うときの「アアルトらしい」柔軟さは、どちらの建物にもまだ見られない。ヴィラ・タンメカンの特徴は居間の暖炉で、図面では壁の端から端まで延びた水平連続窓と背中合わせに配置されている。しかし、このディテールは残念なことに実現されなかった。

アイノとアルヴァ・アアルトは1924年から1927年初めまで、田園都市ユヴァスキュラに建築家ヴィヴィ・ロンが設計したアール・ヌーヴォー精神あふれる一戸建住宅に住んでいた。その後9年間は、トゥルク（1927〜1933年）やヘルシンキの集合住宅に住んだ。1934年に、ほとんど未開発のままの自然が残るムンキニエミのリーヒティエ通りに土地を購入すると、自邸の設計を始め、1936年に完成させた。

リーヒティエ通りの建物は、家族の住居と事務所を兼ねて設計された。それは彼がヘルシンキに実現させた初めての建物で、一種の名刺か、あるいは顧客に示す見本作品の役割を果たした。建物の二つの機能は、外側からもはっきりとわかる。細長い事務所棟は、軽く下塗りして白くのろを塗ったレンガでできていて、材料の構造がそのまま見える。窓の配置にもまだ正統派の機能主義をはっきりと示す特徴がみられる。住居部分の仕上げ材として、ダーク・カラーに着色した細い小割板を使っている。板の継目を不揃いにすることによって、壁の垂直性を和らげようとした。すると、全体としてカーテンのような効果が生まれるのだ。建物は陸屋根で、南に開けた広いテラスがある。

アアルトは多くの著述の中で、建物の内部空間と外部空間の関係に重点を置いて論じている。リーヒティエ通りの家では、南に向いた日当りのよい中庭にできるだけ広い空間を確保するために、建物を可能な限り道路寄りに配置した。道路側のファサードは、かなり閉鎖的で厳格な印象を与えるが、からみつく植物と表玄関へ続く敷石が和らげている。驚いたことに、ドアが「逆に」開くようになっていて、不意をつかれた客に対して、主人が心理的にわずかに優位に立つ。小さな玄関から階段を使って、家族のプライヴェート空間のある上階へ行ける。まっすぐ前方にリヴィング・ルームの眺めが広がり、窓の向こうの中庭まで見通せる。リヴィング・ルームのいっぽうの端には台所と食堂があり、反対側は、二段ほどの階段を上ったところにある事務所を、引戸によって分離している。この建物では、仕事と生活が互いに無理なく連結している。リーヒティエの自邸には、しばしば彼がそう呼ばれている「ロマンティックな機能主義者」という「新しい」一面の徴候がすでに現れている。徴候というのは、仕上げ材としての木の使い方とか、自然石を使った中庭の小道や塀、植物、室内にレンガでつくったオープン・ファイアープレイス、居心地のよいくつろいだ雰囲気のインテリア・デザインなどである。この家は、家具設計や室内装飾に関するアアルト家のイデオロギーを反映していて、それを市場に進出させるために1935年にアルテク社が設立された。

リーヒティエの自邸が、「貧乏な」建築家が自分のために設計した仕事場兼住居としてのささやかな建物であるのに対して、ノールマルックのヴィラ・マイレア（1937〜39年）は、豪奢な邸宅である。フィンランドの古い農家は、シンプルな材料と簡便でやや大ざっぱな建造方法によって、調和のとれた全体をつくりだしているが、アアルトは時々リーヒティエの家をそれと比較した。

いっぽう、ヴィラ・マイレアは明らかに相反する形態と材料と技術、さらに日本のシンプルさと清浄感やフランスの優雅さなど、各国の建築の伝統を表す要素と同じくらい、国際近代主義を暗示する要素にも溢れている。著名な建築史家ウィリアム・カーティスは、「まるで新しいアイディアと手法を試さずにはいられなかったとでもいう感じだ」[19]と書いているが、カーティスと同じく、ヴィラ・マイレアのようなあらゆるものを結合させた構成を待ち望んでいた人は多いだろう。

建物の驚くばかりのパワー――あるいは与える印象――は、相違を魅力的なかたちで捉えている。「ヴィラ・マイレアでは、建築上の不自然な『律動（リズム）』は避けようと努めたが、『形』の方は、それ自体が構造に調和する場合、あるいはそれを通して人々に好感を与えるような性質の材料や仕上げを加えることができる場合は、採り入れた」[20]と、アアルトは説明書に書いている。ヴィラ・マイレアは仕事の接待を兼ねた住居ではあるが、暖かい雰囲気の居心地の良さをさりげなく備えている。

ヴィラ・マイレアはアアルトにとって「愛情を込めた作品」だった。彼は依頼主である友人のマイレとハリー・グリクセン夫妻から自由裁量での設計を任された。費用を気にせずに、何かこれまでになかったような新しい並外れたものをつくってみてはと、励まされさえした。実際アアルトもヴィラ・マイレアのことを、「人々が皆後にその成果を活用できるような一度限りのケース」だと書いている。

ヴィラ・マイレアは、松林の丘の頂きに位置している。建物に近づくときに木々の間から最初に目にはいる光景からは、薄い色合いの近代建築という印象を受ける。もっと近づくにつれ、豊富なディテールと、それらの暗示が効果を発揮し始める。アアルトはしばしば屋外空間と屋内空間の連結地点、来客を中へ通すための中継地点の重要性を力説した。玄関の庇を支える木は、樹皮を残したままかなり密に置かれていて、日中でも光を遮っている。玄関から中へ入るとすぐに、上階へ続く階段に沿って並ぶ「森林」が目に飛び込む。その横に明るく広々とした中庭の眺めが広がる。中庭は湖畔のサウナと石垣のある典型的なフィンランドの湖岸風景を模したミニチュア版だと解釈できる。それに人工の丘を加えて全体が完成している。この庭は、そこで楽しむ以外にも特に鑑賞に適している。

ヴィラ・マイレアとアアルトの自邸の平面図には、多くの共通点がある。両方ともプライヴェート空間を上階に配置し、下階は仕事および接待用の空間にしている。マイレ・グリクセンの絵画アトリエは二階の西端に位置していて、その丸みを帯びた形は、リーヒティエ通りの家と同じように小割板でおおわれている。数々の形態やディテールに、柔らかい曲線を描いた感性豊かな優雅さがうかがえる。近代の工業生産された製品やディテールと並んで、熟練した手作業のディテールもあちこちに見られる。

アアルトの代表作の一つであるヴィラ・マイレアは、形態や材料から始まって、様々な手法や潜在意識の中の夢想に至るまで、彼の建築のすべてのレパートリーあるいは「登場人物」が、それぞれの役を担った一つの劇のようである。その作風は、合理的、非合理的、空想的、感情的、有機的、その他にでも順次変化してゆく。

アアルトはヴィラ・マイレアにおいて、住宅設計の手腕を独特のやり方で、またあらゆる面で一度に見せることができた。いっぽう同じ頃、社会の住宅生産とコミュニティ・プランが、彼の仕事の中で重要な位置を占めるようになった。大規模な工業地域計画は、1930年代に都市計画から個々の労働者住宅へと広がっていった。その10年間、特に1940年にアメリカのMITで教鞭をとった頃、タイプ住宅の問題と規格化の可能性及び必要条件を研究した。

フィンランドに帰国すると、現実の住宅問題に直面した。戦争で家を失った50万の避難民が、新しい住処（すみか）を必要としていたのだ。今から考えれば、アアルトはやがて来る戦争と、その結果を予測していたのではないかとさえ思

える。それほどまでに彼の案は時宜にかない、深く考え抜かれていた。
根底にある考えは、柔軟性のある規格化と大量生産だった。つまり住宅そのものではなく、建物の各部を規格化するべきだということだ。[21]そうすれば、その時々のニーズに合わせて主空間の周りに丸太の枠組みを一室づつ付け足していくカレリア地方の伝統的な建造方法のように、成長し、変化する柔軟な空間をつくることができるだろう。1940年のアアルトのAA-住宅は、このイデオロギーの上にたった素晴らしい一例である。一つの基本タイプから69種にも変形できるのだ。それが美術館であろうと小住宅であろうと、柔軟性という条件はアアルトの建築の一つの要である。
アアルトのタイプ住宅は、フィンランドのあちこちの工場住宅地区におよそ2000戸ほど建てられた。だが柔軟な規格化の方針は、それ以上活用されることなく終わった。経済の見通しが、より多く大量生産できてなおかつ安価な解決策の方に味方したからだ。

戦争中と1940年代末のフィンランドは緊縮経済の時代で、建築家も設計の仕事がわずかしかなかった。40年代の終わりに、ヘルシンキ工科大学とセイナッツァロの役場とユヴァスキュラ教育大学のコンペティションに勝って以来、上昇気流に乗るアアルトの新しい局面が開け始めた。セイナッツァロの役場(1949〜1952年)は、国際的に通用する傑作になった。赤レンガ、木、銅が、今や彼が使う主材料である。形態世界に入ってきたのは、古代様式と中世の地中海地方の建築で、アアルトは己の建築にとって無尽蔵ともいえる源泉を、それらの中に見いだした。

規格住宅を数に入れなければ、ヴィラ・マイレアの次に設計した一戸建住宅は、ムーラッツァロに建てた実験住宅と呼ばれるアアルト家のサマー・ハウス(1952〜1954年)である。最初の妻アイノが他界したのが1949年で、その後、彼はセイナッツァロのプロジェクトに加わった若い建築家エルサ(エリッサ)・マキニエミと1952年に再婚した。実験住宅は二人のための「田舎の隠れ家」になり、人を招くことはめったになかった。

セイナッツァロの南に位置する島ムーラッツァロは、アアルトにとって、今世紀初めからすでに馴染みの地域だった。1903年に一家がユヴァスキュラに引っ越してきたとき、アルヴァは山と森と湖が支配する内陸部の景色に初めて出会った。公務員と教師が多いこの町では、当時すでに別荘文化と水上交通が生活に入り込んでいた。

実験住宅は、湖の水面から突き出た巨大な岩ののり面に建っている。周りの自然条件も手伝って、建物の釣り合わせと基礎の技術的な試みが実験された。初期段階で建てたレンガ部分は外側が白く粗塗りされ、後に、白く塗った木造の客室棟が林の斜面に建てられた。ギリシャ神殿と自然との関係を思わせるような大胆な建物の配置が、フィンランドの緑の森を背にしてなされている。

白い外観と対照をなしているのが、中庭の赤レンガの温もりだ。彼は中庭の壁面を50ヵ所に区分して、様々なレンガの質と組積工法における耐久性と視覚的効果を試してみた。種々のレンガを敷いた中庭を支配しているのが、中央に配されたオープン・ファイアープレイスだ。レンガの間からは緑色の苔と白いクローバーが生え出ている。

建物内の各室は、中庭を囲む二つの棟に分配されている。北側の棟には仕事部屋と結合したリヴィング・ルームがあり、屋根裏にアアルトの絵画用アトリエをつくっている。東側の棟は寝室になっていて、北棟との連接部分にキッチンと洗面所が置かれ、さらに巧みに設計された通廊が客室棟とつないでいる。

物理的にだけでなく、解釈の上でも実験住宅はなかなか近づきにくい建物である。アアルト建築の基本要素が、ここでは数多く見いだされる。アアルトはよく屋外と屋内空間の境界を取り払ったが、この中庭は、その優雅で精巧な手法を示す格好の例だろう。リヴィング・ルームから中庭を通して湖への視界が開け、寝室の窓からは庭の向こうの西壁に設けた開口部の遥かかなたに、ムーラ

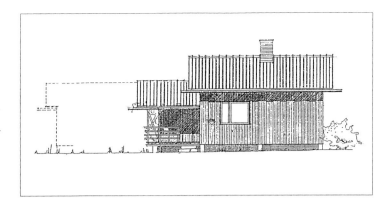

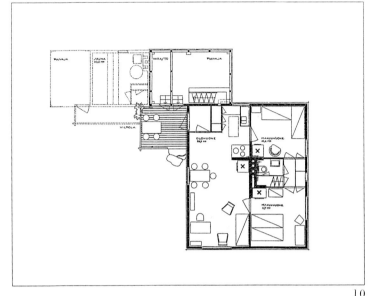

10. *Standard house, elevation and plan, 1941.*

10. スタンダード・ハウス、立面と平面、1941。

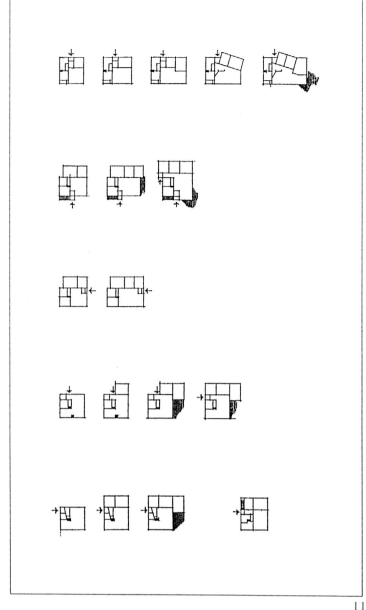

11. *Variants of the AA-House series, 1941.*

11. AAハウスのヴァリエーション、1941。

メ教会の塔（アルヴァ・アアルト設計、1926〜1929年）がかすかに見える。いっぽう台所からは、二つの窓と通廊の向こうに北の斜面が広がる。普段はその斜面を通って客がここにやって来るのだ。

実験住宅には、明らかにロマンティックな古代の精神が漂っている。分離して建つ外壁と開口部は、何かかつて存在し破壊されたもの、廃墟のノスタルジアを暗示している。しかしながら建物の歴史的広がりというのは表面的な借用ではなく、潜在意識の中の暗示枠に隠され、縛られている。ウィリアム・カーティスは、それを「隠れた存在」[22]と表現している。

ヴィラ・マイレアとムーラッツァロの実験住宅は、真面目で肯定的な意味での「遊び」と、実験という点でつながっている。両方ともそれぞれ強力な独自性（アイデンティティ）を持っている。背景として、一種の家族の相似が見受けられる。厳密に定めた様式概念や、あらかじめ規定した枠内にアアルトの建物を当てはめるのは、実際不可能である。

パリから50kmほど離れたバゾッシュ・シュール・グイヨンヌにあるメゾン・カレ（1956〜1961年）もまた、多分に主観的な建物である。それが誕生した過程自体が、すでに多くの建築的解釈法の理由を物語っている。パリの美術商ルイ・カレは、自分に家を設計してくれる腕のいい建築家を誰か知らないかと、スウェーデン人の友人に訊ねた。そうしてアルヴァ・アアルトの名前が彼の耳に入り、手紙のやりとりをした後、アアルトが設計したビエンナーレのパヴィリオンがオープンするヴェネツィアで、1956年夏に面会しようという約束がまとまった。初対面で、両氏の間には早くも終生の友情が生まれた。カレとアアルトは二人とも赤ワインに目がなく、芸術及び文化界の仲間との国際的交流が日常生活の一部になっているという共通点もあり、すっかり意気投合したのだ。

メゾン・カレはヴィラ・マイレアと同じく、仕事とプライヴェートな生活を兼ねた住宅である。費用の限度を考えずに自由にアイディアを実現させるチャンスを、アアルトは再び手にしたわけだ。中央に位置するエントランス・ホールを囲むように、それぞれ異なる機能を持つ各室が分類して置かれ、見たところ明快で細胞の集まりのようである。ホールのフリーフォームの高い木製天井は、ヴィープリの図書館を思わせる。気持ちの上ではほとんど神聖といえるこの空間に、玄関ドア上方の横窓からわずかに陽光が差し込む。壁面には美術品が飾られ、床には彫刻が数点置かれている。

エントランス・ホールから幅の広い階段を降りると、リヴィング・ルームにつながる。壁いっぱいの窓には、芝庭の眺望が大きく広がる。現在、この庭はうっそうとした森に縁どられている。ここでも再びアアルトは、暗から明へ、また屋根の自然な傾斜にそって高いレヴェルから低いレヴェルへと、訪問者を巧みに誘導する。「パブリック・スペース」としては、さらにリヴィング・ルームの横に位置する書斎を兼ねた図書室と、エントランス・ホールの後ろに隠れるようにして静けさを保つ食堂がある。

プライヴェート空間と客室は建物の南側に配置され、直接自然につながっている。それらの部屋の入口は、エントランス・ホールを分割する「美術品を飾る仕切壁」で巧妙に隠されている。彼はこれと同じ手法を、後にロヴァニエミのアホ邸でも使った。使用人の部屋は二階にある。

メゾン・カレは白漆喰を塗ったレンガづくりの建物で、北側ファサードを支配する二方向へ緩く傾斜した屋根には、抽象的でかすかにではあるが、フランク・ロイド・ライトのプレーリー・ハウスや、アアルトの1940年代のいくつかの一戸建住宅に相通じるものが見られる。屋根が交差する部分に、内側に入り込んだ玄関を配置している。自然石は地元産の砂岩である。南側ファサードはもっと彫刻的で、その均整（プロポーション）には、特にムーラッツァロの実験住宅につながる要素がある。

メゾン・カレは、端々まで建物のすべてが「アアルト流」の芸術作品である。たくさんの細かなディテールも、パブリック・スペースの家具や照明器具の大部分も、この住宅のためだけに丁寧にデザインされた。エリッサ・アアルトが

手伝った痕跡もあちこちに見られる。ここでも庭がまるで内部空間の続きのようで、段状の斜面が、下方にあるスイミング・プールに向かって少しずつ下降線を描き、その後、自然の森へと続いている。建った当時は、外壁のすぐ前から小さな葡萄畑が広がっていた。

1960年代になるとアアルトの建築は、より彫刻的でモニュメンタルな形態言語へと転向していった。後の作品を見てみると、ときどき折衷的な、さらにはバロックの様相さえ呈している。けれども数少ない個人住宅では、自分なりの流儀を保持した。彼が住宅を設計するのは友人にだけで、彼らの個性や仕事が建物に明確な特徴を与えている。

コッコネン邸（1967〜1969年）は、フィンランド・アカデミーの仲間である作曲家ヨーナス・コッコネンのために設計した住宅である。設計の出発点は、作曲家にとって最も大切な道具であるグランド・ピアノで、それが他の部屋の条件を左右した。実際、仕事部屋は鉛の防音引戸によって他の部屋から分離されており、音響に細心の注意が払われている。また建物の他の部分よりも高く立ち上がっている。壁面と床の大部分と構造には木が使われていて、リーヒティエのアアルトの自邸と同じように、外壁に小割板が施されている。

この住宅には、めったにないほどの暖かさと静けさが漂っている。建物は木々の間に隠れ、明確なファサードというものがない。母屋から下方のサウナまで屋根が続いている。考えるまでもなく頭に浮かぶのは、森で偶然出会って初めて気付くような、昔のフィンランドの山荘だ。中に入ると家の性格がはっきりと表れる。まるで各部がそれぞれの場所に納まった、繊細なオルゴールのようなのだ。同様の感覚をスンマのエンソ・グートツァイト社管理者の家の居間にも採り入れている。

コッコネン邸の内向的な表現と対照をなすのが、存在そのものを率直に誇るようなシルツ邸（ヴィラ・シェッペット／1969〜1970年）だ。この住宅は、アアルトの伝記の著者である親友ヨーラン・シルツのために設計された。アアルトはこれを建てることによって、シルツをフィンランドに留まらせたかったのだ。シルツ邸では、他の建物部分よりも高い位置になるように、リヴィング・ルームを車庫の上に載せ、この家特有の性格を強調した。建物マッスに、ヴィラ・マイレアやリーヒティエの家と共通する点がはっきり見られる。さらに航海の趣味を持つこの作家の海上生活を暗示する要素も認められる。現にそれは海への眺望が開ける船橋のようだ。建物の背後には、中央にフリーフォームの睡蓮の池を配した親しみやすい中庭があり、反対側の端を縁どるように小さな客室棟が建っている。

見たところ平面計画に硬さがあるにもかかわらず、シルツ邸にはアアルトらしい優雅さがある。多様な形の空間は、小さな薄暗いエントランスから階段を二つ分上った明るいリヴィング・ルームへとスムーズに流れる。食堂は、ムーラッツァロの実験住宅やティーリマキのアトリエ、オクサラ邸と似た手法で、台所の隣に分離して配置されている。

一戸建住宅は、アルヴァ・アアルトの広範な作品群の中でも、多彩で魅力的な一群を形成している。その室内建築を特徴づけているのは、パブリックとプライヴェートの明確な分離である。多くの場合、彼のリヴィング・ルームは典型的な接待用空間で、家具に至るまで慎重にデザインされている。いっぽう、家族が日常集まる場所は、たいていキッチンの隣に配置されたダイニング・ルームである。アアルトの一戸建住宅にはすべて、暖炉が少なくとも一ヵ所以上あり、内部空間の構成上それは欠かせないものだ。それらは時にはリーヒティエやムーラッツァロの場合のように、縮小されてシンプルなこともあるが、たいてい造形的な彫刻のようで、空間の要の部分につくられている。

アアルトの一戸建住宅からは、彼の建築の概要と、1920年代から1970年代にかけての変化を見てとることができるが、同時にほとんどすべての作品に、彼独特の流儀も見受けられる。たとえば、小さな建物は周りの環境にしっかりと結びついている。彼はしばしば内部空間の延長、ある種の中継空間を外に向けてつくることによって、自分の理想に沿った環境を形づくったからだ。また、サウナやその他の離れ家を中庭の周りに集めるという、古くから我が国で行われてきた方法を使って、囲われ護られた居心地のよい中庭をつくり出すことも多かった。

建築に関するアアルトの著述では、「小さな人間」と「自然」という言葉が何度も繰り返し使われている。彼に関しては、生態学の概念が生まれるずっと以前から、生態学的建築を扱ってきたといえるだろう。1940年にアアルトはこう書いている。
「建築家の仕事は、未来から過去までの糸を一つに結び合わせながら調和をつくりだすことに尽きる。その根底にあるのは、無数の感情の糸を持つ人間と、（人間を含む）自然である」[23]

＊註は22頁英文を参照

Notes

1. Alvar Aalto, "Saunatemppeli", *Keskisuomalainen*, 22. 1. 1925. ("Temple Baths on Jyväskylä Ridge", Göran Schildt, *Alvar Aalto in his Own Words*, Keuruu 1997)
2. Alvar Aalto, "Suurten mittojen arkkitehti", *Seura*, 28. 6. 1944.
3. Göran Schildt, ". . . But you can set it an example", *Alvar Aalto in his Own Words*, Keuruu 1997.
4. Alvar Aalto, "Arkitekternas paradistanke", *Föredrag vid Syd Sveriges Byggmästarsällskaps jubileumsmöte i Malmö* 1957. ("The Architect's Dream of Paradise", Göran Schildt, *Alvar Aalto in his Own Words*, Keuruu 1997)
5. Avar Aalto, "Menneiden aikojen motiivit", *Arkkitehti*, 1992. ("Motifs from Past Ages", Göran Schildt, *Alvar Aalto in his Own Words*, Keuruu 1997)
6. "Journey to Italy", Göran Schildt, *Alvar Aalto in his Own Words*, Keuruu 1997. Interview in Casabella Contunuità 1954.
7. Alvar Aalto, "Porraskiveltä arkihuoneeseen", *Aitta* no. 1 1926. ("From Doorstep to Living Room", Göran Schildt, *Alvar Aalto in his Own Words*, Keuruu 1997).
8. Kirsi Saarikangas, "Model Houses for Model Families. Gender, Ideology and the Modern Dwelling", *The Type-Planned Houses of the 1940s in Finland*, Helsinki 1993.
9. Town hall was a study project. Never realized.
10. Alvar Aalto, "Eliel Saarinen", Göran Schildt, *Alvar Aalto in his Own Words*, Keuruu 1997.
11. See e. g. Kirmo Mikkola, "The transition from classicism to functionalism in Scandinavia", *Classical Tradition and the Modern Movement*, Helsinki 1985.
12. Alvar Aalto, "Asuntomme probleemina", *Domus*, 1930. ("The Housing Problem", Göran Schildt, *Alvar Aalto in his Own Words*, Keuruu 1997)
13. Alvar Aalto, "Uusimmista virtauksista rakennustaiteen alalla", *Uusi Aura* 1. 1. 1928. ("The Latest Trends in Architecture". Göran Schildt, *Alvar Aalto in his Own Words*, Keuruu 1997)
14. Alvar Aalto, "Rationalismi ja ihminen", *Esitelmä Ruotsin Taideteollisuusyhdistyksen vuosikokouksessa* 1935. ("Rationalism and Man", Göran Schildt, *Alvar Aalto in his Own Words*, Keuruu 1997)
15. ibid.
16. Alvar Aalto, "The Humanizing of Architecture", *The Technological Review*, November 1940. (Göran Schildt, *Alvar Aalto in his Own Words*, Keuruu 1997)
17. ibid.
18. See e. g. Beatriz Colomina, *Privacy and Publicity: Modern Architecture as Mass Media*, The MIT Press, Cambridge Mass. 1996, and Colin St. John Wilson, *The Other Tradition of Modern Architecture: The Uncompleted Project*, Academy Editions, London 1995.
19. William Curtis, "The Idea of Modern Tradition". *Functionalism—Utopia or a Way Forward*, Jyväskylä 1992.
20. Aino ja Alvar Aalto, "Mairea". *Arkkitehti* no. 9, 1939. ("The Villa Mairea", Göran Schildt, *Alvar Aalto in his Own Words*, Keuruu 1997)
21. Alvar Aalto, "Euroopan jälleenrakentaminen", *Arkkitehti* 1941. ("The Reconstruction of Europe is the Key Problem for the Architectural of Our Time", Göran Schildt, *Alvar Aalto in his Own Words*, Keuruu 1997)
22. William Curtis, ibid.
23. Alvar Aalto, "The Humanizing of Architecture", *The Technological Review*, November 1940. (Göran Schildt, *Alvar Aalto in his Own Words*, Keuruu 1997)

1920-1940

Note: All scales in the captions indicate the reduced scale in this issue.

註：キャプション中の縮尺はすべて誌面上の縮尺率を示す。

House for Terho Manner, Töysä, Finland, 1923

Villa Vekara, Karstula, Finland, 1924

Aalto's Own House and Studio, Riihitie, Helsinki, Finland, 1934-1936

Residence for Manager, Sunila Pulp Mill, Kotka, Finland, 1936-1937

House for Chief Engineer, Tampella Mill, Inkeroinen, Finland, 1937

Villa Mairea, Noormarkku, Finland, 1937-1939

House for Terho Manner
Töysä, Finland 1923

マンネル邸
フィンランド、トゥーザ　1923

In 1923, Alvar Aalto designed a house in Töysä near Kuortane, where he was born, for Terho Manner, a relative who was a surveyor. It consisted of a main building like a manor house, with outbuildings.
The house is a textbook design example, reflecting the young architect's newly adopted Palladian and Baroque themes. The walls of one room on the upper floor were left in their natural log finish as an homage to the vernacular tradition.

1923年、アアルトは、彼の郷里クオルタネの近郊トゥーザにテルホ・マンネル氏のための住宅を設計した。マンネル氏は彼の親戚にあたり、測量技師であった。住宅は、荘園邸宅風のメインの建物と外部の付属の建物で構成される。
この住宅は、若い建築家が新たに取り入れたパラディアン様式やバロック様式を反映する教則本的一例である。二階にある一部屋の壁は、丸太木の自然な仕上げのまま残されているが、それは地域の伝統にたいして敬意を払ったものである。

Right: Site plan, scale: 1/1500.
Opposite: Symmetrical facade consisting of a main building with outbuildings.

配置図。縮尺：1/1500。右頁：メインの建物と付属施設が左右対称に構成されたファサード。

Opposite: Main facade, winter season, view from lake side (east). Above: Details of window and door of outbuilding.

左頁:湖畔側から見る冬の風景。上:付属施設の窓、ドアなど建具のデザイン。

Above: Bedroom on 2nd floor with natural log finish. Opposite: Staircase at entrance hall.

上：2階の寝室。壁は自然の木質がいかされている。右頁：エントランス・ホールにある階段。

This small log villa was commissioned in 1924 by a school friend of Alvar Aalto, an engineer named Karstu. The floor plan of the building is 5.7 × 7.7 metres. The numerous detail drawings that have been preserved in the archives show how carefully the building was designed and it is indeed one of the best preserved works of Aalto's Classical period. The furniture was commissioned at the same time, but was not designed by Aalto.

この小さな木造の住宅は、アアルトの学友でカルツという名のエンジニアが1924年に委託したものである。建物の平面は5.7m×7.7mである。アアルト財団の資料庫に保管されている多くのディテール図面が、いかにこの建物が注意深く設計されたか、そしてこれがアアルトのクラシカル時代における作品の最も良い保存状態のものであることを示している。家具もまた同時代に注文されたものであるが、アアルトのデザインではない。

Right: Site plan, scale: 1/1500.
Opposite: Facade of entrance. Finished by traditional red ochre paint.

右：配置図。縮尺：1／1500。右頁：入口側のファサード。赤色の仕上げは伝統的な塗料を用いている。

Above: Looking to the north terrace from lake side. Below: Terrace. Opposite: Staircase and baluster.

上：北側のテラスを湖畔側から見る。
下：テラス。右頁：階段と手摺子のデザインを見る。

Aino and Alvar Aalto moved to Helsinki in 1933. They acquired a site for their own home and office in Helsinki's Munkkiniemi in 1935, and the building was finished in 1936.
(See text on p.10)

1933年にアイノとアルヴァのアアルト夫妻はヘルシンキへと移住した。1935年、彼らはヘルシンキのムンキニエミに自邸とスタジオのための敷地を手に入れることができた。建物の完成はその翌年の1936年である。(詳しくは論文18頁参照)

Right: Site plan, scale: 1/800.
Opposite: General view of the south facade.

右：配置図。縮尺：1/800。右頁：南側の全景。

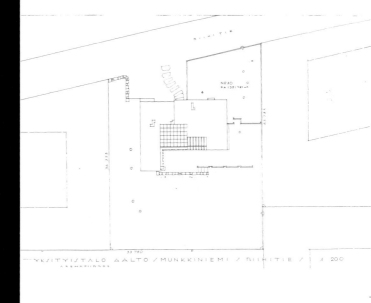

pp.36–37: Looking from south courtyard. The whitewashed brick wing at left is Aalto's office. The black stained timber wing at right is his house. Above: View to the west corner of the studio with V-shaped roof (see drawing 3.9). Opposite: Access to the entrance. Stepping stones were also designed by Aalto.

36～37頁：南側の中庭から見る全景。左手の白く仕上げられた棟はスタジオに、右手の黒く着色された木造の棟は自邸となっている。上：Ｖ字型の屋根勾配を持つスタジオを西側より見る（図面3.9参照）。右頁：エントランスへのアクセス。飛び石もアアルトによって計画されている。

pp.40–41: Living room with large window facing south courtyard. Above: Studio with gallery. Opposite: Dining room. Drawings on the wall are by Aalto.

40〜41頁:南の中庭に面する大窓のある
居間。左頁:ギャラリーのあるスタジオ。
上:食堂。壁に掛かったドローイングも
アアルトによる。

The house was built as a part of the extensive factory and residential area, where building was begun in 1936 and continued right up to the 1950s. The house contains about fifteen rooms, kitchens, terraces and balconies. The house still belongs to Alvar Aalto's Functionalist period, although there are hints of what was to come in some of the details, such as the wood paneling.

この住宅は、スニラ製紙工場の広大な工場と職員住宅地域の一角に建てられた。全体計画は、1936年に始まり、1950年まで続けられた。この住宅は約15の居室と台所、テラス、そしてバルコニーからなる。この住宅は、木のパネルなどいくつかのディテールにおいて、この先アアルトの作品がどのように展開されていくかというヒントがあるが、まだアアルトの機能主義時代に属している。

Right: Site plan. Opposite: North entrance facade.

右：配置図。右頁：北側のエントランス・ファサード。

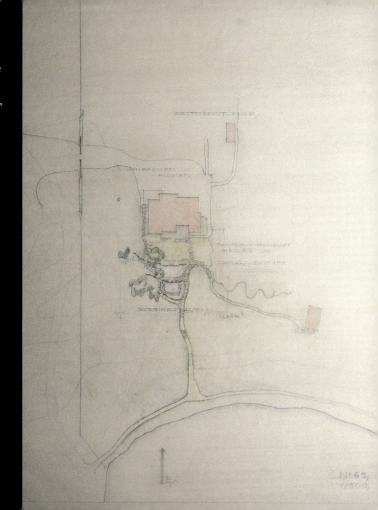

Above: South facade facing the courtyard. Opposite: View to the west wing from terrace.

上：中庭に面した南側ファサード。右頁：テラスより西側の棟を見る。

Opposite: Living room facing south courtyard. Above: Detail of rattan-clad pillar.

左頁：南側の庭に面した居間。上：藤材で仕上げをした柱のディテール。

Above: Staircase. Opposite: Hall on 2nd floor. Veranda seen through the window.

上：階段。右頁：2階廊下。西側のヴェランダが窓越しに見える。

In 1937 Aalto designed three houses for Tampella engineers in the Inkeroinen mill area. The white rendered houses have steeply pitched roofs. The floor plan of the chief engineer's house follows the pattern that Aalto had already used in his own house, with the 'public' spaces, dining room, living room and study forming a comprehensive spatial sequence on the lower floor. The position of the open hearth in the entrance hall is exceptional in Aalto's one-family houses. Upstairs the bedrooms are grouped around a hall.

1937年、アアルトはタンペラ社のインケロイネンにある製紙工場エリアに3棟の技術者のための家を設計した。白く塗られた住宅はそれぞれ急勾配の屋根を携えている。この主任技術者の家の平面は、アアルトが自らの住宅で使用したパターンに準じている。それは、「公的」空間、食堂、居間、書斎が下の階で分かりやすいシークエンスを形成しているということである。エントランス・ホールにある暖炉の位置は、アアルトの住宅作品の中では例外的なものである。上階の寝室は

Opposite: Upward view from east side. The house seen in the distance is also designed by Aalto. Above: Composition of roof, chimneys and veranda.

左頁：東側からの見上げ。奥にある住宅もアアルトの設計である。上：屋根、煙突、ヴェランダのコンポジション。

Above: Twilight view from street side. Opposite: Entrance hall with fireplace.

上：通り側から見る夜景。右頁：暖炉の あるエントランス・ホール。

Above: Hall on 2nd floor facing the veranda onto street. Opposite: Sauna dressing room.

上：通り側のヴェランダに面した2階ホール。右頁：サウナの脱衣所。

Alvar Aalto prepared the first design for the Villa Mairea in the winter of 1938. Work started on the basis of a second design drawn up in the spring, but Aalto changed the drawings again in the summer when the foundations were already finished. The last drawings are dated January 1939 and the house was largely complete in the late summer/early autumn of 1939.
(See text on p.10)

1938年冬、アアルトはヴィラ・マイレアのための最初のデザインを用意していた。工事は、翌春に仕上がっていた第二段階の基本設計に従って進められたのだが、アアルトは夏になって再び図面を描き替えてしまった。そのときは建物の基礎はほとんどできあがっていたのだった。最終の図面の日付は1939年1月となっていて、この住宅が概ね完成したのはその年の晩夏もしくは初秋のことだった。(詳しくは論文18頁参照)

Right: Site plan, scale: 1/800.
Opposite: View of the garden side over the pool. Projection in front is the sauna diving board.

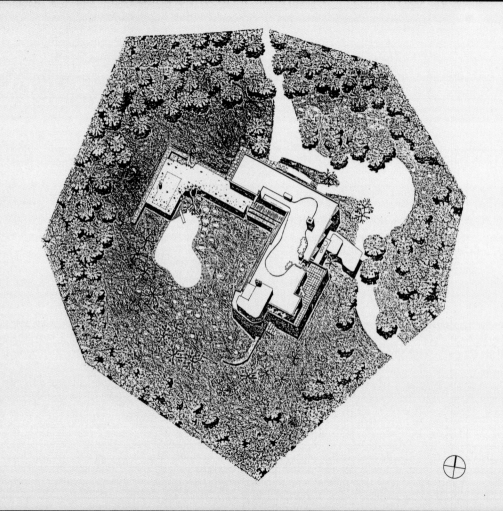

pp.62–63: Looking to entrance facade through pine forest.
pp.64–65: General view from inner court which could be construed as a typical Finnish lakeside landscape in miniature. Above: Northeast facade giving the impression of a Modernist building. Opposite: Detail view of bay windows.

62〜63頁：松林の向こうに南側のエントランス・ファサードを見る。64〜65頁：中庭側の全景。典型的なフィンランドの湖畔の風景を坪庭のように表現しているとも解釈できる。上：モダニズムの印象を与える北東側全景。右頁：出窓のディテール。

Opposite: Night view of entrance. Above left: Capital detail of column supporting entrance canopy. Above right: Detail of entrance door.

左頁：エントランス夜景。左上：エントランスのキャノピーを支える柱の柱頭ディテール。右上：エントランスの扉のディテール。

Above: Entrance hall with free-form wall. Opposite: Looking to living room from entrance hall.

上：フリーフォームの壁があるエントランス・ホール。右頁：エントランス・ホールより居間を見る。

pp.72-73: Living room with organic shaped fireplace and rattan-clad pillars. Opposite: Staircase in living room. Above: Looking to staircase over the screen wall between entrance hall and living. Experimental relief for hybrid chair made of laminated wood is in the center.

72〜73頁：有機的な曲線の暖炉、藤仕上げの柱などがデザインされた居間。左頁：居間にある階段。上：エントランス・ホールと居間を仕切る壁越しに階段を見る。中央はハイブリッド・チェアのための木材の積層合板による実験的レリーフ。

*Above: Corner of the living room.
Opposite: Wintergarden with
bamboo fittings and rattan
furnishings giving a Japanese
impression.*

上：居間の南西隅部分。右頁：竹の建具、
藤家具など日本を彷彿させるウインター
ガーデン。

Library with corrugated wall. Light can be seen radiating from its slits.

波型の壁のある書斎兼図書室。スリットから光が放射状に広がる。

*Cabin-like studio on 2nd floor.
p.80: Curved wall detail of
fireplace in living room.*

船室のような2階のアトリエ。80頁：居間にある暖炉の湾曲した壁のディテール。

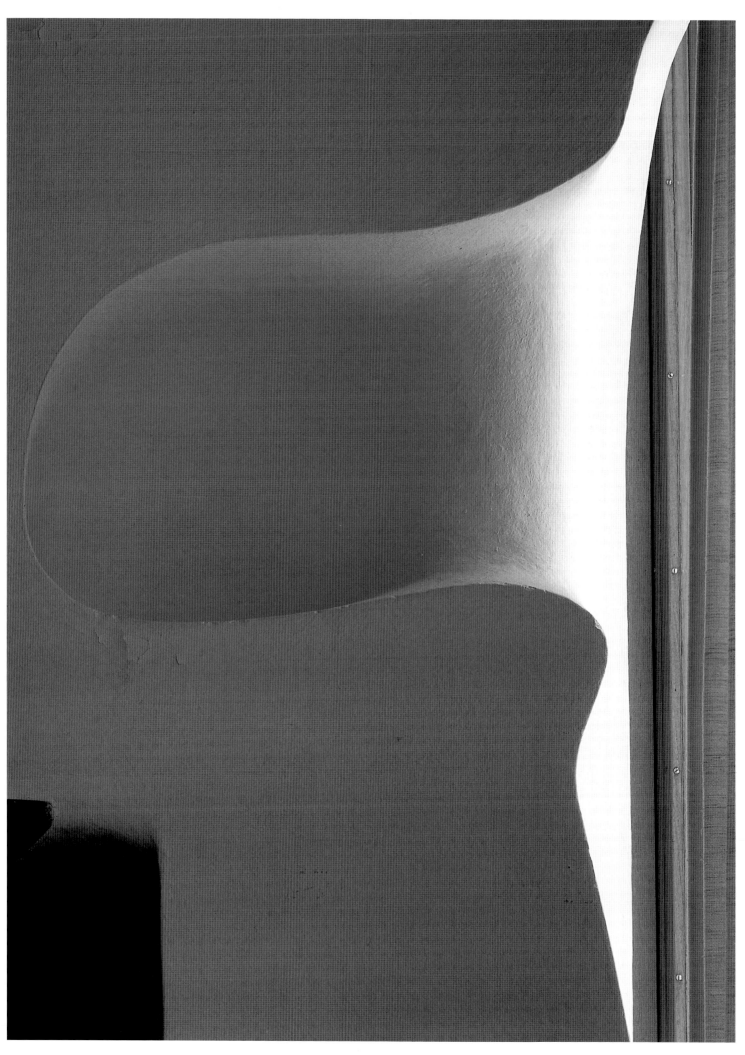

1. House for Terho Manner / マンネル邸

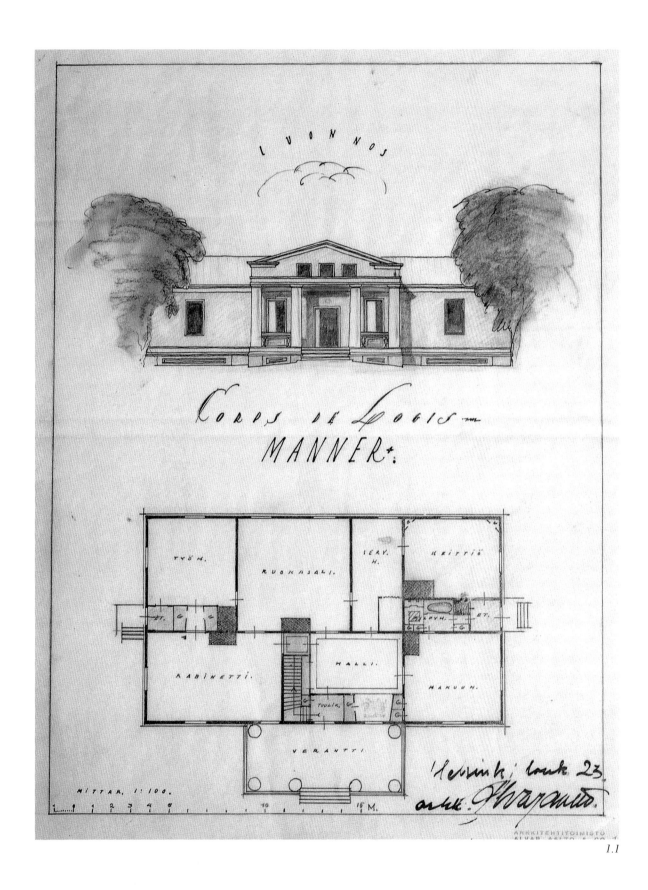

1.1

1.1: Elevation and plan.
1.2: Elevation of main building, scale: 1/150.
1.3: Drawing of sauna, scale: 1/300.

1.1：立面と平面図。
1.2：母屋の正面立面図。縮尺：1/150。
1.3：サウナ棟の平・立・断面図。縮尺：1/300。

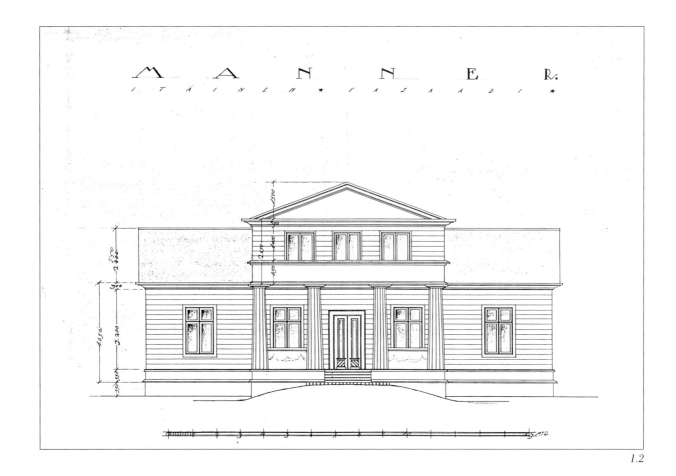

1.2

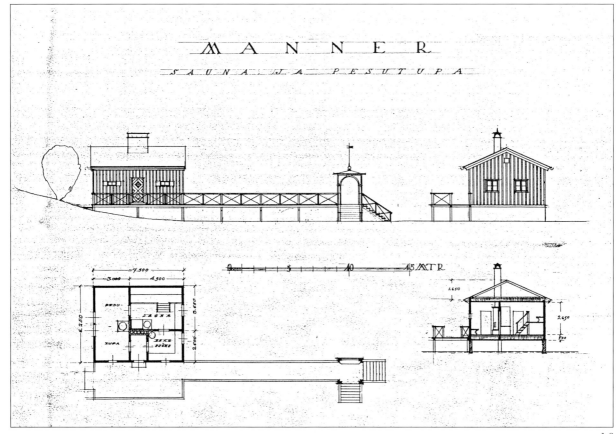

1.3

2. Villa Vekara / ヴェカラの夏の家

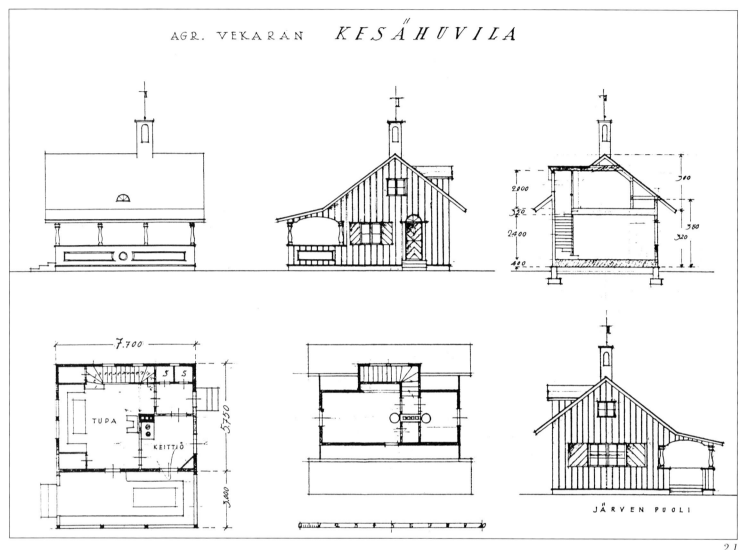

2.1

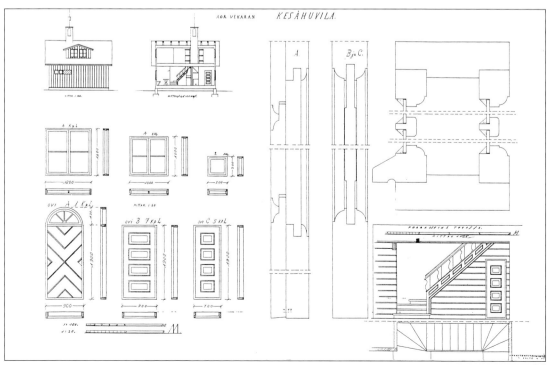

2.2

2.1: Plans, elevations, and short section, scale: 1/200.
2.2: Details of fittings and stair.

2.1：1、2階平面図、立面図、短手方向断面図。縮尺：1/200。
2.2：建具、階段周りの詳細図。

3. Aalto's Own House and Studio / アアルト自邸とスタジオ

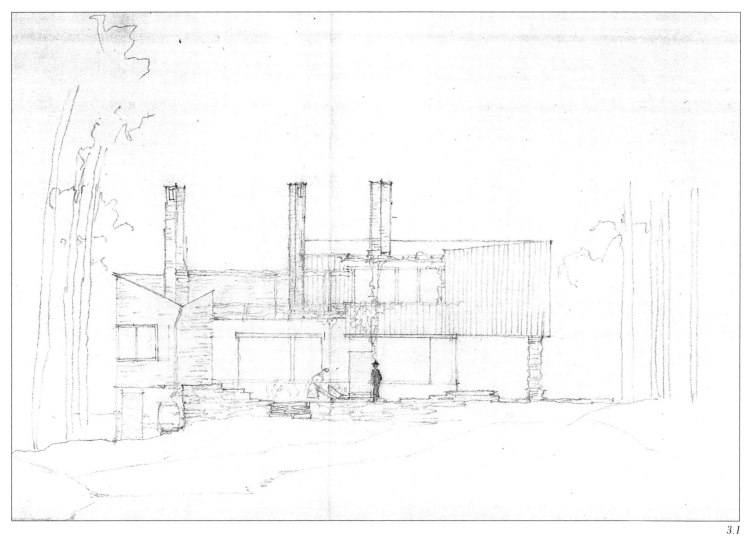

3.1

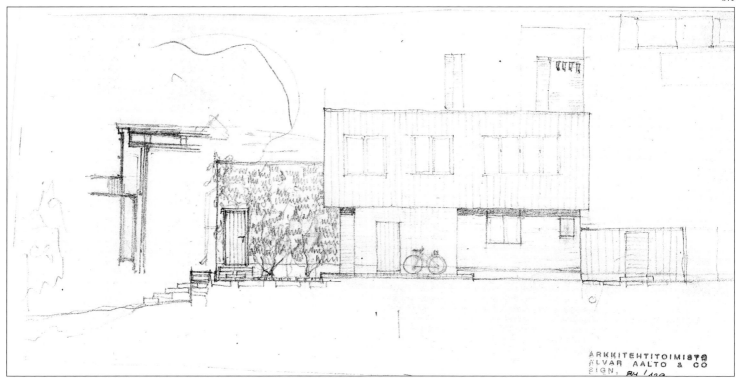

3.2

3.1: Sketch of garden facade.
3.2: Sketch of east facade.
3.3: 2nd floor plan and ground floor plan.

3.1：庭側ファサードのスケッチ。
3.2：東側面のファサードのスケッチ。
3.3：1、2階平面図。

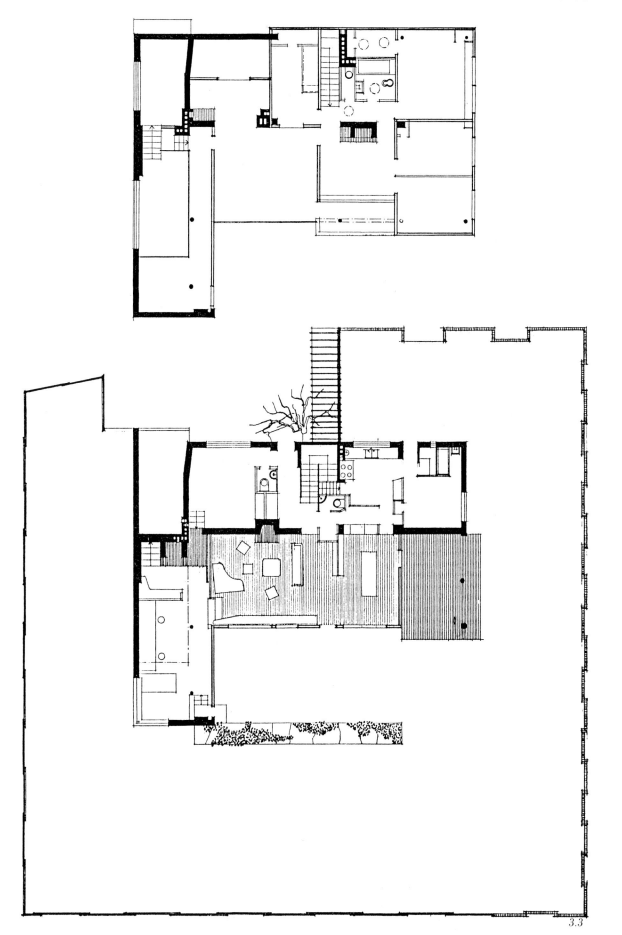

3.3

3.4: Site plan and planting design.
3.5: Short section through living room, scale 1/200.
3.6: Elevation of street side (northeast), scale 1/200.
3.7: Elevation of garden side (southwest), scale 1/200.

3.4：敷地計画図と植栽計画図。ナナカマドなどの樹木が計画されている。
3.5：居間を通る短手方向断面図。
3.6：通り側（北東）立面図。
3.7：庭側（南西）立面図。

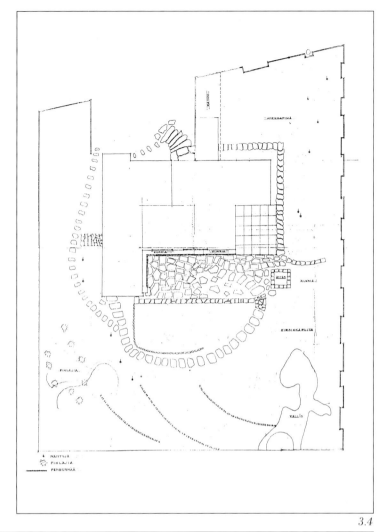

3.4

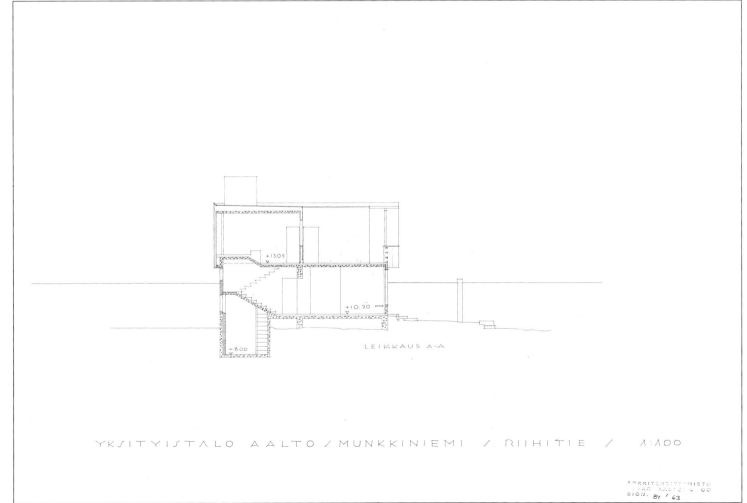

3.5

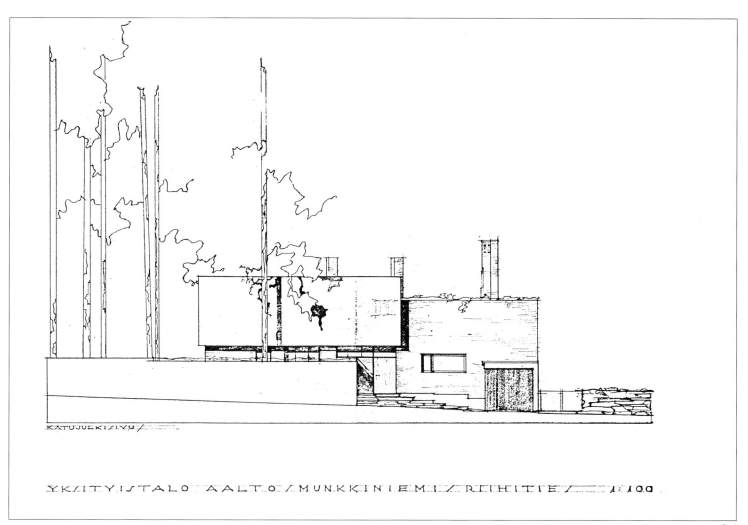

3.6

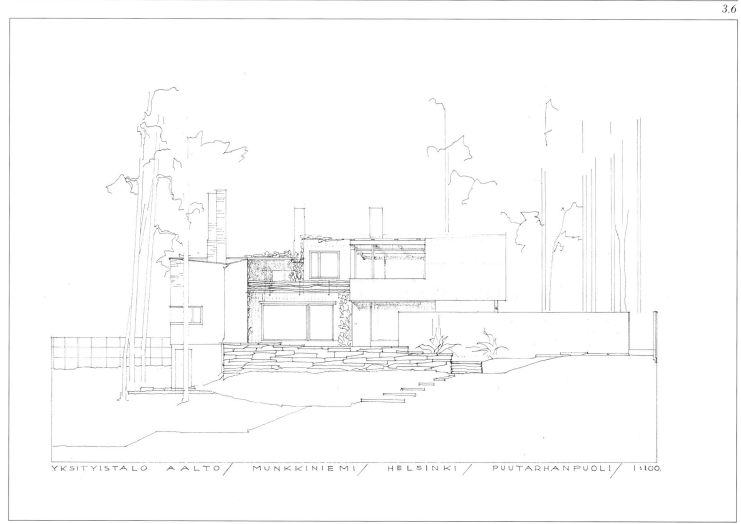

3.7

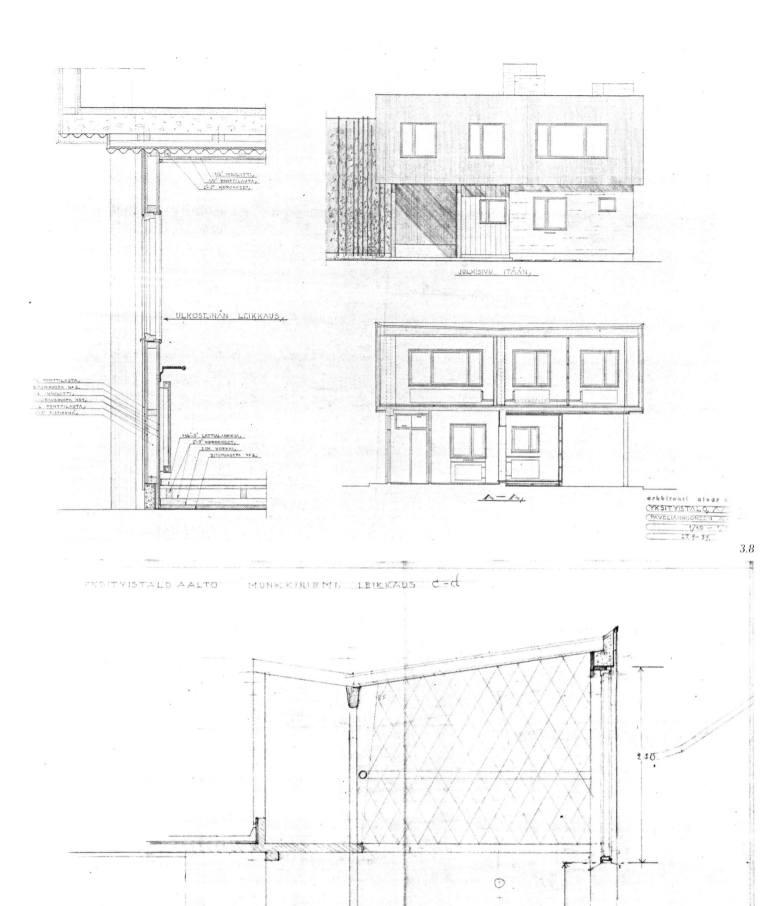

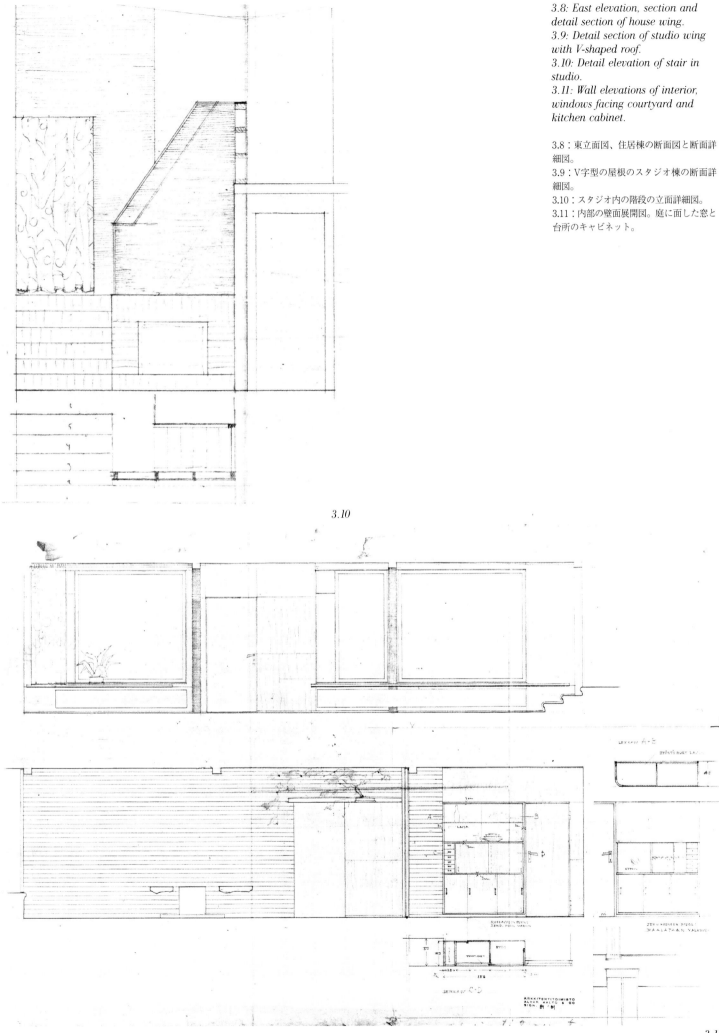

3.8: East elevation, section and detail section of house wing.
3.9: Detail section of studio wing with V-shaped roof.
3.10: Detail elevation of stair in studio.
3.11: Wall elevations of interior, windows facing courtyard and kitchen cabinet.

3.8：東立面図、住居棟の断面図と断面詳細図。
3.9：V字型の屋根のスタジオ棟の断面詳細図。
3.10：スタジオ内の階段の立面詳細図。
3.11：内部の壁面展開図。庭に面した窓と台所のキャビネット。

3.10

3.11

4. Residence for Manager, Sunila Pulp Mill / スニラ製紙工場管理者の家

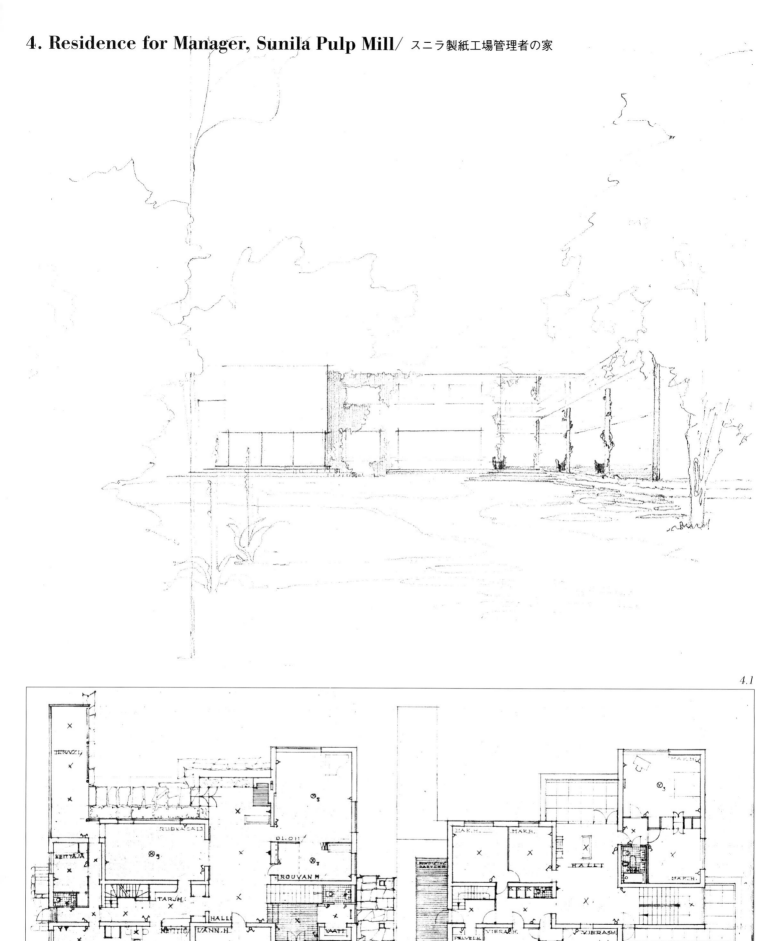

4.1: *Sketch of south facade and courtyard.*
4.2: *Plans from planning stage.*
4.3: *South elevation, scale: 1/200.*
4.4: *West elevation, scale: 1/200.*
4.5: *North elevation, scale: 1/200.*
4.6: *Ground floor plan, scale: 1/200.*

4.1：南側ファサードと中庭のスケッチ。
4.2：計画段階の平面図。
4.3：南立面図。縮尺：1/200。
4.4：西立面図。縮尺：1/200。
4.5：北立面図。縮尺：1/200。
4.6：1階平面図。縮尺：1/200。

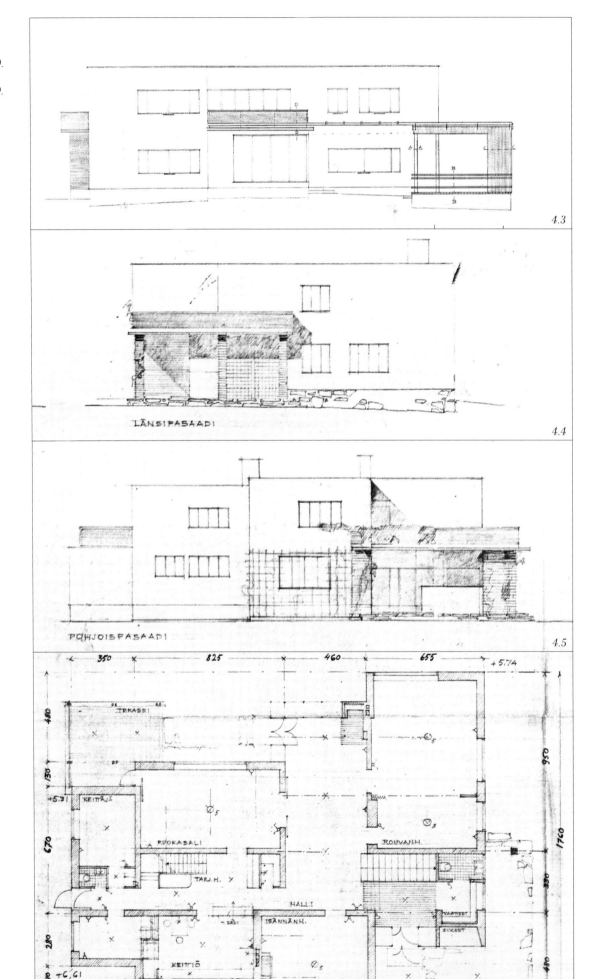

5. House for Chief Engineer, Tampella Mill / タンペラ製紙工場主任技術者の家

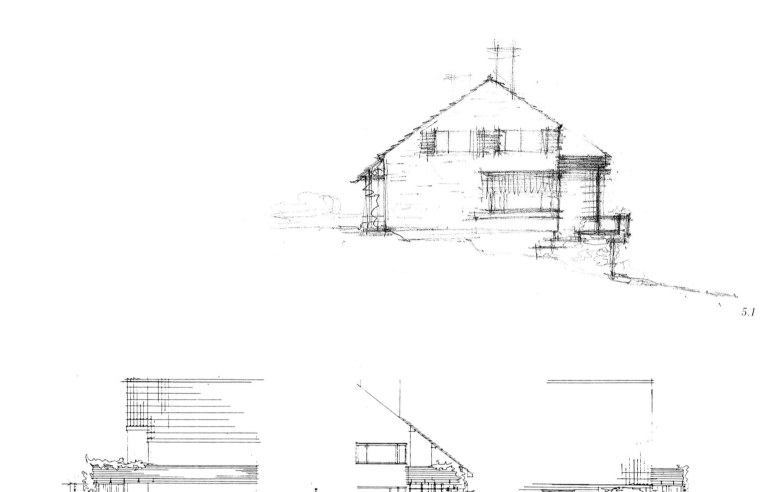

5.1

5.2

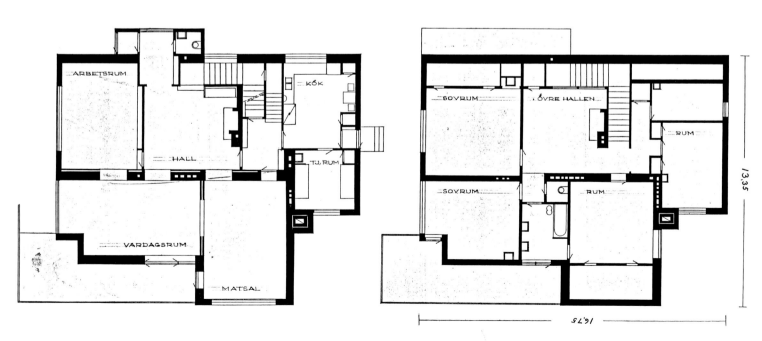

5.3

5.1, 5.2: Sketches of facade.
5.3: Entrance floor plan (left) and upper floor plan, scale: 1/200.
5.4: East elevation, scale: 1/200.
5.5: South elevation, scale: 1/200.
5.6: Short section, scale: 1/200.

5.1、5.2：ファサードのスケッチ。
5.3：エントランス階平面図（左）と上階平面図。縮尺：1/200。
5.4：東立面図。縮尺：1/200。
5.5：南立面図。縮尺：1/200。
5.6：短手方向断面図。縮尺：1/200。

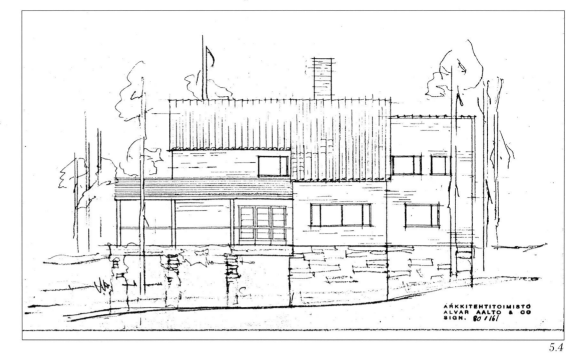

5.4

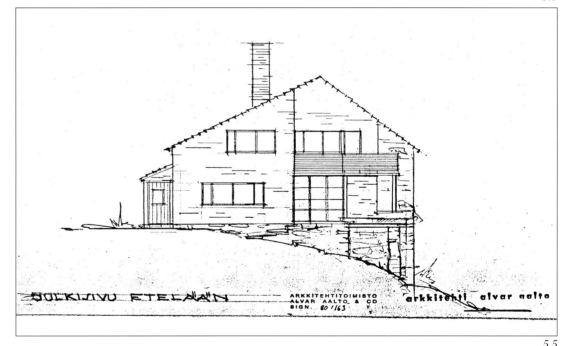

5.5

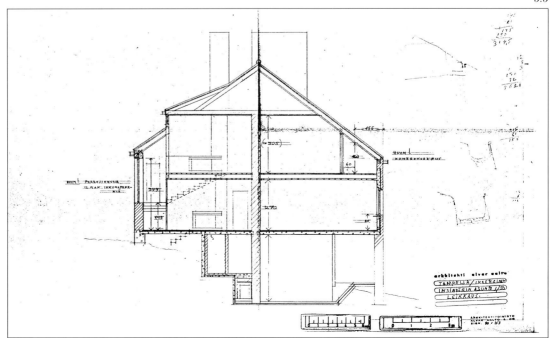

5.6

6. Villa Mairea / ヴィラ・マイレア

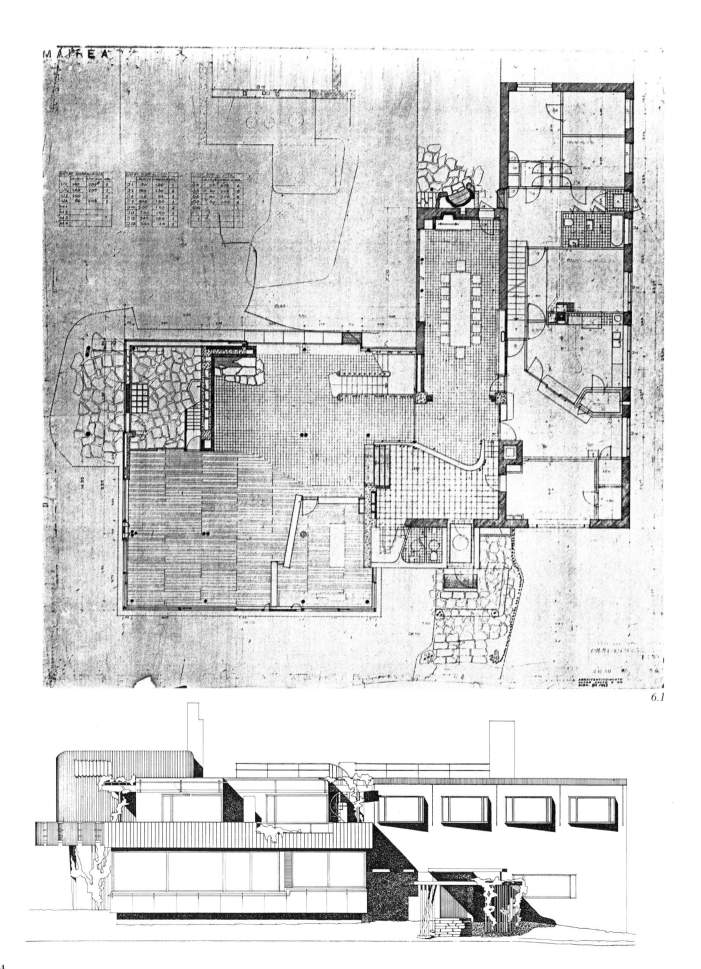

6.1

6.3

6.1: Ground flooor plan, scale: 1/200.
6.2: 2nd floor plan, scale: 1/200.
6.3: Entrance (southeast) elevation, scale: 1/200.
6.4: Garden (northwest) elevation, scale: 1/200.

6.1：1階平面図。縮尺：1/200。
6.2：2階平面図。縮尺：1/200。
6.3：入口側（南東）立面図。縮尺：1/200。
6.4：庭側（北西）立面図。縮尺：1/200。

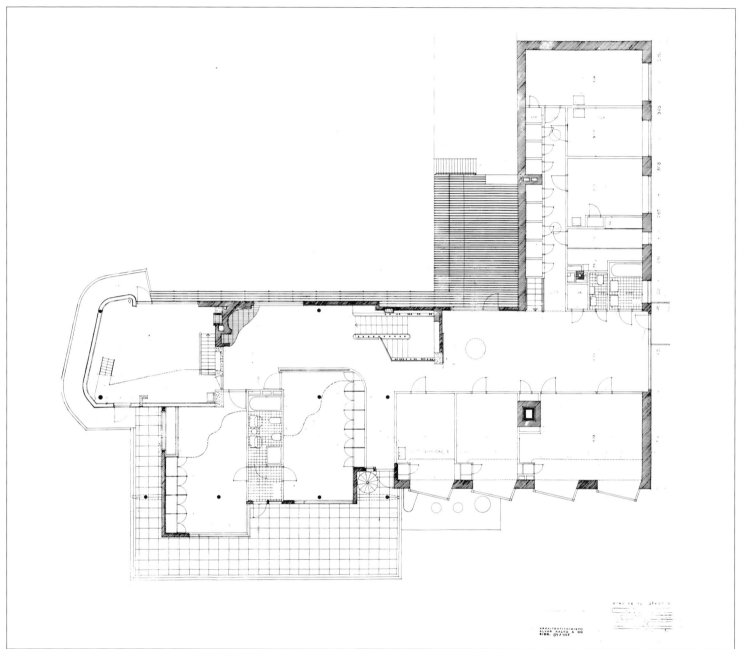

6.2

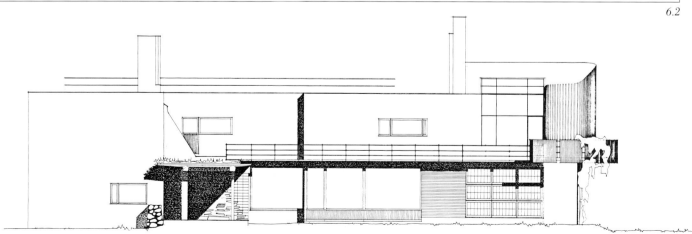

6.4

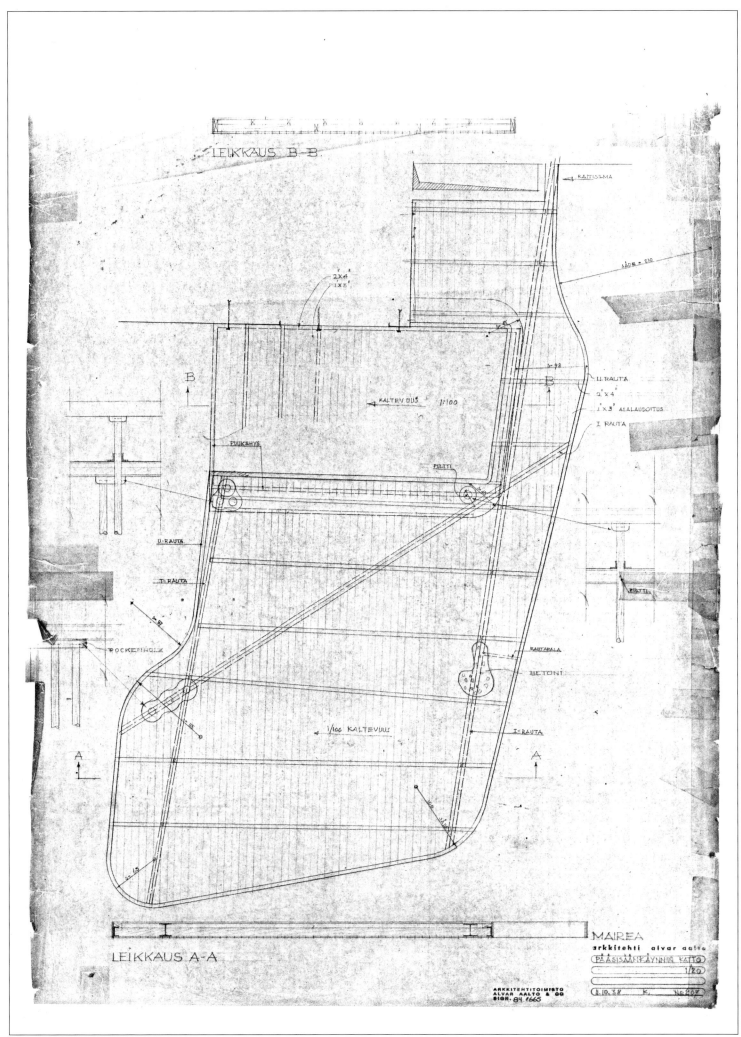

6.5: Ceiling plan of entrance canopy.
6.6: Side detail elevation of entrance.
6.7: Detail of fireplace of dining room, view from outside.

6.5：エントランス・キャノピーの天井伏せ図。
6.6：エントランスの側面詳細図。
6.7：食堂の外部暖炉の詳細図。

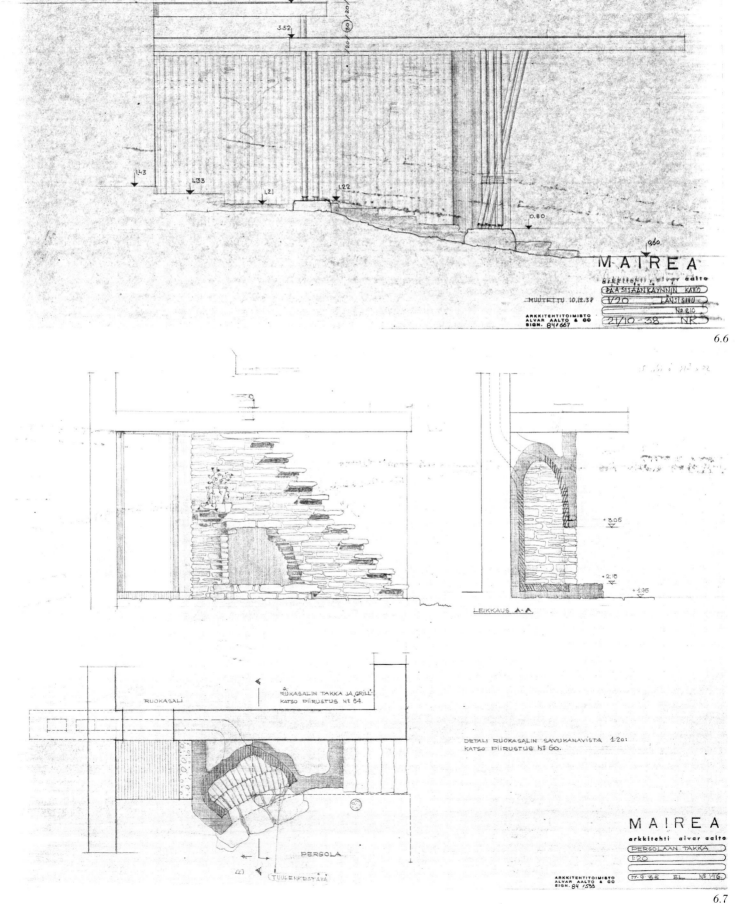

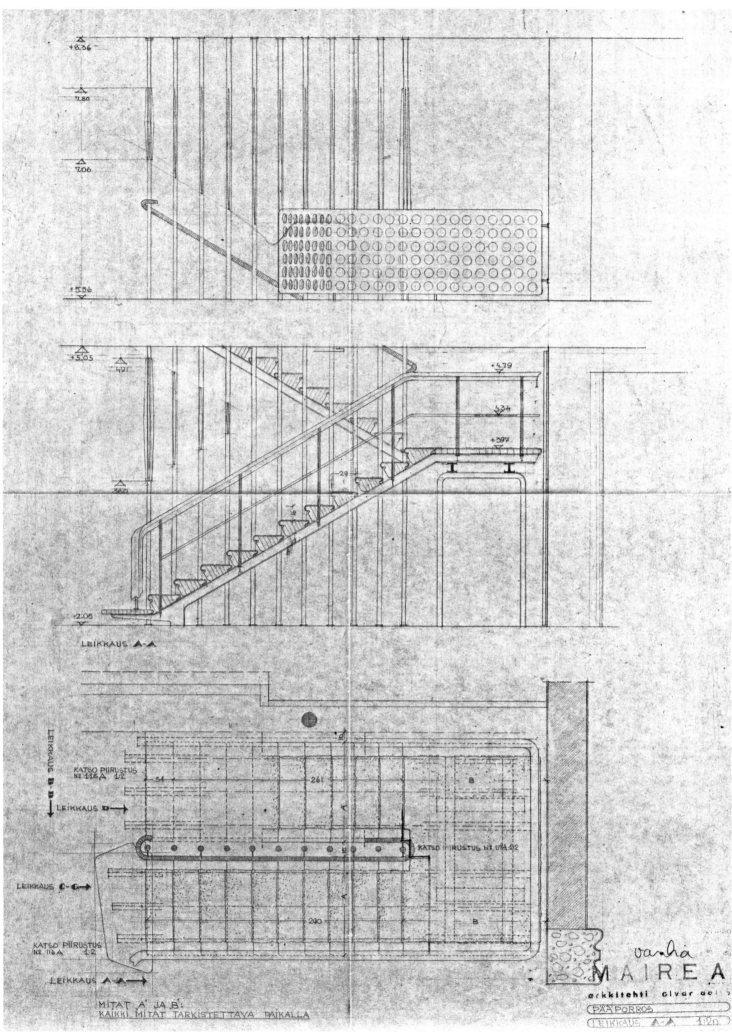

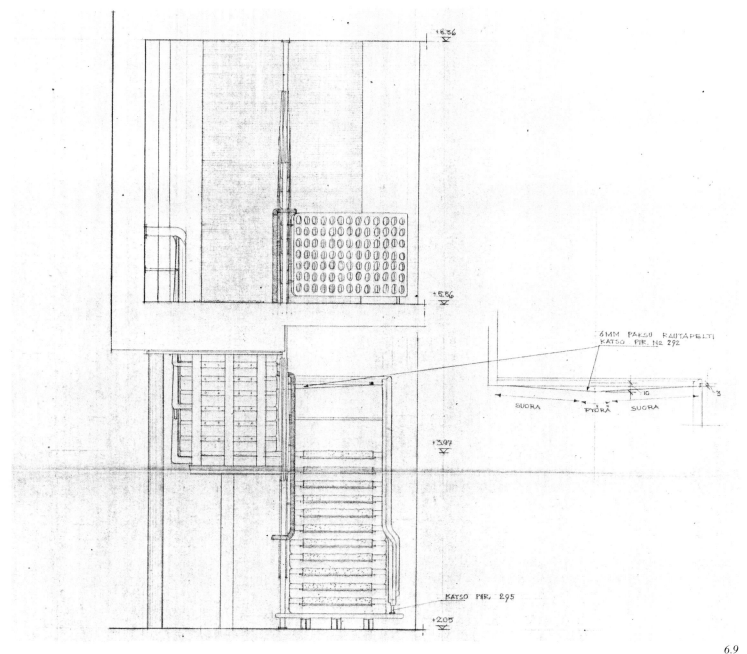

6.9

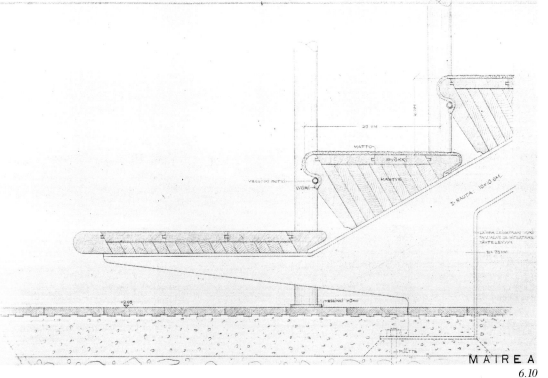

6.10

6.8: Side elevation and plan of staircase in living room, from planning stage.
6.9: Facade of staircase in living room, from planning stage.
6.10: Detail section of footboards.
6.11: Detail of corrugated wall of library.
6.12: Detail of rattan-clad column and cedar-clad column.

6.8：居間の階段の側面図と平面図。
6.9：居間の階段の正面図。
6.10：階段踏み板の詳細断面図。
6.11：書斎の波型スリット入り欄間の詳細図。
6.12：藤仕上げの柱と杉仕上の柱の詳細図。

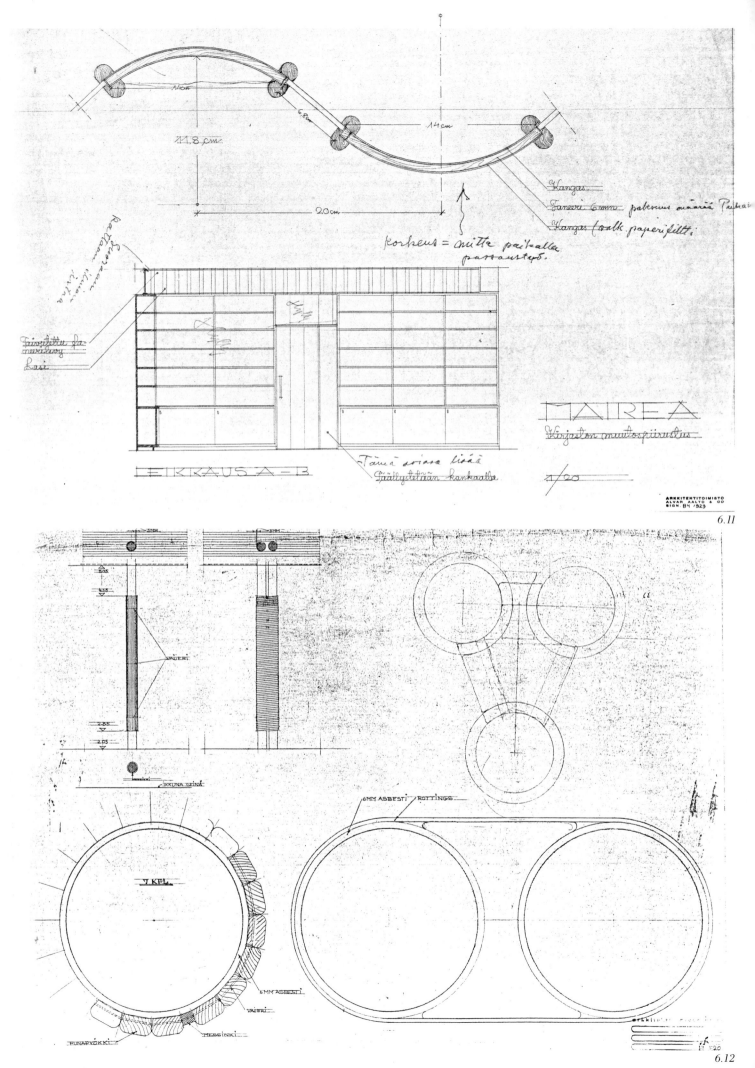

1941-1960

House for Site Manager, Ahlström, Pihlava, Finland, 1946

Experimental House, Muuratsalo, Finland, 1952-1954

Maison Carré, Bazoches-sur-Guyonne, France, 1956-1961

Manager's House B, Enso-Gutzeit, Summa, Finland, 1959-1960

Manager's House C, Enso-Gutzeit, Summa, Finland, 1959-1964

In 1942 Aalto drew up plans for managers' houses to be built on various industrial estates. Closely related to Aalto's standard one-family houses for officials, the managers' houses have a square floor plan and a hipped roof. The house has a horizontal emphasis overall, influenced perhaps, by Frank Lloyd Wright. Some houses of this type were erected in the 1940s.

1942年、アアルトはこの住宅の平面をあらゆる工業団地に建てられるように描いた。アアルト設計の労働者のための一般的な個人住宅と密接な関係があり、この管理者の家は正方形の平面形を持ち、寄せ棟づくりとなっている。全体的に水平性を強調していて、おそらくフランク・ロイド・ライトに影響されたものであろう。このタイプの住宅が何件か1940年代に建てられている。

Right: Site plan, scale: 1/1500.
Opposite: Twilight view from lake side.

右：配置図。縮尺：1/1500。右頁：湖側から見る夕景。

*Above: General view from south.
Opposite: General view from north street side. It has a hipped roof reminiscent of Frank Lloyd Wright.*

左頁:南側(湖側)から見る全景。上:
北側(通り側)から見る全景。寄せ棟屋
根がF・L・ライトの影響を思わせる。

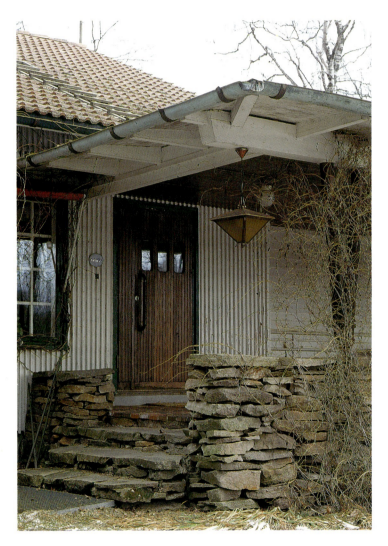

Above: Entrance porch of the lake side. Opposite: Living room.

上：湖側のエントランス・ポーチ。右頁：居間。

During the construction of Säynätsalo Town Hall, Alvar and Elissa Aalto (who were married in 1952) discovered an attractive site on the island of Muuratsalo, some 5 kilometres to the south. There they designed and built a summer house and studio for leisure and architectural experiments.
Since 1994 the house has been maintained by the Alvar Aalto Museum.
(See text on p.11)

セイナッツァロ村役場の工事中に、アルヴァ・アアルトと2番目の妻エリッサ（1952年に結婚）は、その敷地より5km南のムーラッツァロ島に魅力的な敷地を見つけた。彼らはその場所に夏の家兼スタジオをレジャーと建築的実験のために設計し竣工させた。この作品は、1994年からアルヴァ・アアルト美術館の管理となり、手入れされている。（詳しくは論文19頁参照）

Right: Site plan. Opposite: Twilight view from the courtyard to the lake. The wall frames the view.

上：配置図。右頁：中庭より湖を見る。壁が景色の中にフレームをつくっている。

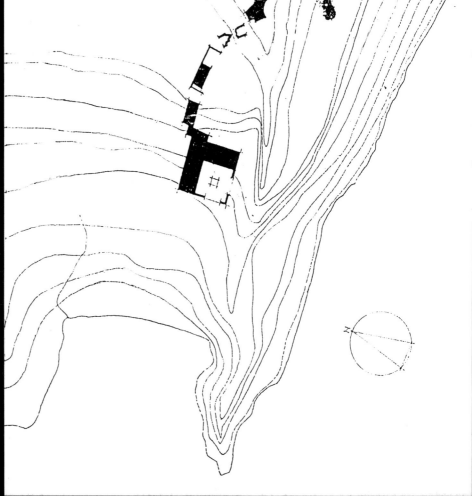

pp.110-111: South wall looking from the courtyard. Experimental brickwork and tiles are shown.
pp.112-113: General view from rearside. Opposite: Looking from the north. Above: Courtyard wall details.

110〜111頁：中庭より南壁面を見る。実験的な煉瓦積みやタイル貼りが見られる。112〜113頁：背面からの全景。左頁：北側より見る。上：中庭の壁面詳細。

*pp.116-117: Dining and living room. Opposite: Looking to studio from living. The gallery was also designed as a studio.
Above: Diagonal view from gallery.*

116〜117頁：食堂兼居間。左頁：居間からスタジオを見る。ギャラリーもスタジオとして設計されている。上：ギャラリーからの見下ろし。

Above left: Sauna at lakeside. Above right: Detail of sauna entrance. Opposite: Harbor of the original approach.

左上：湖畔のサウナ。右上：サウナ入口の詳細。右：建設当時使用されていたアプローチのための船着き場。

In 1956 Alvar Aalto had a second opportunity to design a luxury residence, the Villa Mairea having been the first. Maison Carré was designed as the home of the wealthy art dealer and diamond merchant, Louis Carré. At the same time it had to function as a place for meeting special clients and showing precious stones. Besides the house, Aalto was commissioned to design all the interior furnishings and the external areas, complete with swimming pool, terraces and vineyard.
(See text on p.12)

1956年、アアルトはヴィラ・マイレア以来の二度目の高級住宅設計の機会を得た。この住宅は、美術・宝石商の富豪ルイ・カレ氏の自宅として設計された。それと同時に特別な顧客と会合をもち、貴重な石を見せるための場としても機能しなければならなかった。住宅そのものと同時に、アアルトはインテリアの家具やプール、テラス、ぶどう畑を含む外構の

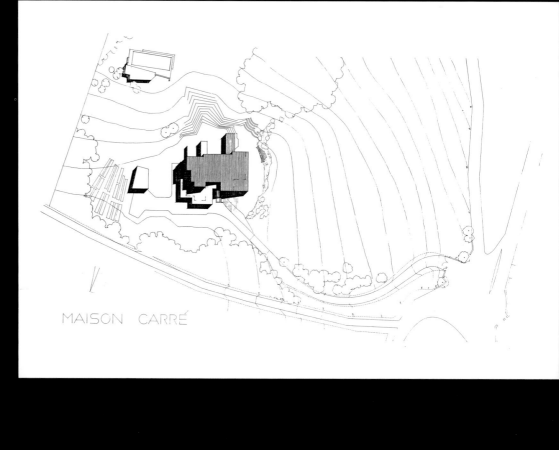

MAISON CARRÉ

pp.124–125: General view from the south. The terraced slopes lead down to the swimming pool. Above: Looking from the east. Opposite: Looking from southeast.

124〜125頁：南側から見る全景。テラス状の階段がプールへと導く。左頁：東より見る。上：南東より見る。

Opposite: Detail view of outside porches in the south garden. Above: West end of gutter along the roof slope and a drain.

左頁：南側の庭のポーチの詳細。上：屋根勾配に沿って設けられた樋の西端と雨落ち。

Above: Inside of pool side pavilion.
Opposite: Pool and pool side pavilion.

上：プール・サイドの東屋内部。右頁：プールとプール・サイドの東屋。

Above: Interior of living room. Opposite: Entrance hall with curved ceiling made of pine. "Artwork wall" in the center is dividing the hall and guest rooms. (Sectional detail of the hall shown in drawing 9.9).

上：居間内部。右頁：湾曲した松材の天井を持つエントランス・ホール。中央の美術品の展示壁が客間とホールを隔てている（断面詳細図は図面9.9参照）。

Manager's House B, Enso-Gutzeit
Manager's House C, Enso-Gutzeit
Summa, Finland 1959-1960, 1959-1964

エンソ・グートツァイト社管理者の家B棟
エンソ・グートツァイト社管理者の家C棟
フィンランド、スンマ　1959〜1960、1959〜1964

Manager's house for Enso-Gutzeit, B, 1959–1960

In this house, set into a steep slope, Aalto has placed the 'public' spaces, living room, library and dining area upstairs and the private rooms downstairs. The building is of white rough-cast brickwork and dark-stained timber. Today the house functions as a company guest house.

エンソ・グートツァイト社管理者の家B棟
急勾配の敷地に建つこの住宅の中に、上階には居間、書庫、食堂を、下階には個人の部屋をアアルトは配置した。白く粗塗りされた煉瓦と黒く着色された木材でこの住宅はつくられている。現在は会社のゲスト・ハウスとして使用されている。

Manager's house for Enso-Gutzeit, C, 1959–1964

The second manager's house, located next door to the first one, was designed with a much freer approach and has a slightly fan-shaped plan form. The 'public' spaces here too, are upstairs and the private ones downstairs. The finest detail in the house is the stepped timber ceiling in the living room.

エンソ・グートツァイト社管理者の家C棟
前掲のエンソ・グーツァイト社の管理者の家の隣にこの管理者の家は建てられた。前作よりも自由なアプローチとやや扇型の平面形が用いられた。ここでもまた、公的空間は上階に、私的空間は下階に設けられた。この住宅の中で最もすばらしいディテールは、居間の階段状の木造天井である。

Right: Site plan, scale: 1/1500. According to original site plan, three houses are named A, B and C from the north.

右：配置図。縮尺：1/1500。オリジナルの配置図に従って、北からA棟、B棟、C棟。

Manager's House B, Enso-Gutzeit
エンソ・グートツァイト社管理者の家B棟

pp.136-137: General view from north. Above: Downward view from east street side. Opposite: South facade. pp.140-141: Living room on upper floor.

136〜137頁：北側からの全景。上：東の通り側からの俯瞰。右頁：南ファサード。140〜141頁：上階の居間。

Manager's House C, Enso-Gutzeit
エンソ・グートツァイト社管理者の家C棟

pp.142-143: Looking to the west side. Above: Northwest exterior corner of living room. Below: West facade view. Opposite: Detail of entrance of east side. (Ceiling plan and detail shown in drawing 11.7).

pp.146-147: Living room with stepped timber ceiling on upper floor. (Section shown in drawing 11.6). p.148: Hall on upper floor.

142～143頁：西側を見る。上：居間の北西隅外観。下：西側ファサード、夏の風景。右頁：東側のエントランス（天井伏せ図は図面11.7参照）。

146～147頁：上階の階段状の天井を持つ居間（断面図は図面11.6参照）。

148頁：上階のホール。

7. House for Site Manager, Ahlström / アハルストリョム社管理者の家

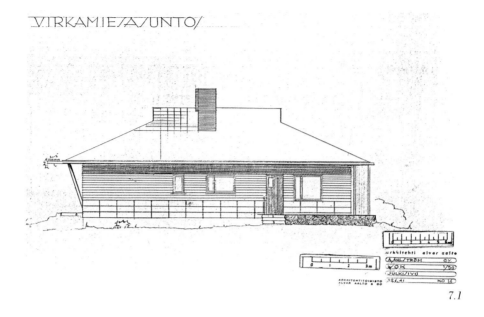

7.1

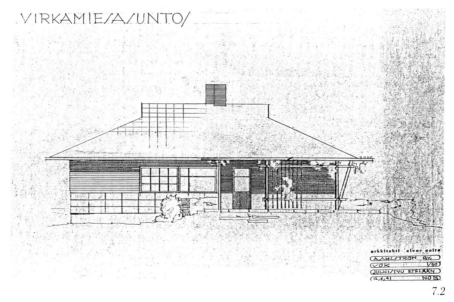

7.2

7.3

7.1: Street side (north) elevation, scale: 1/200.
7.2: Lake side (south) elevation, scale: 1/200.
7.3: Street side elevation, from planning stage, scale: 1/200.
7.4: Plan, scale: 1/200.
7.5: Diagram of building environment.
7.6: Detail of entrance porch.

7.1：通り側（北）立面図。縮尺：1/200。
7.2：湖側（南）立面図。縮尺：1/200。
7.3：計画段階の北立面図。縮尺：1/200。
7.4：平面図。縮尺：1/200。
7.5：建築を取り囲む周辺環境の図解。
7.6：エントランス・ポーチの詳細図。

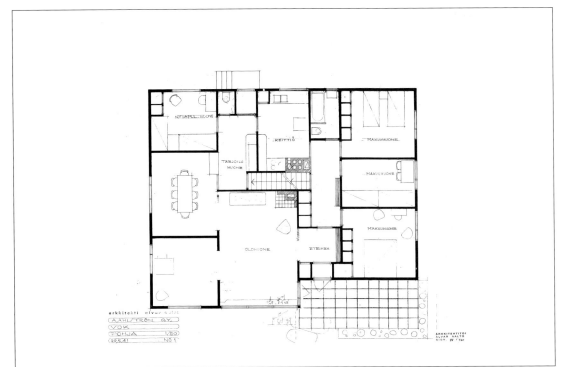

7.4

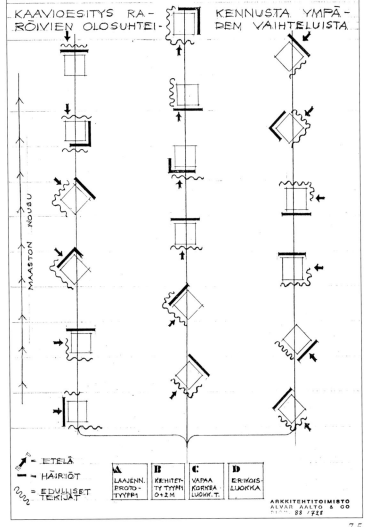

7.5

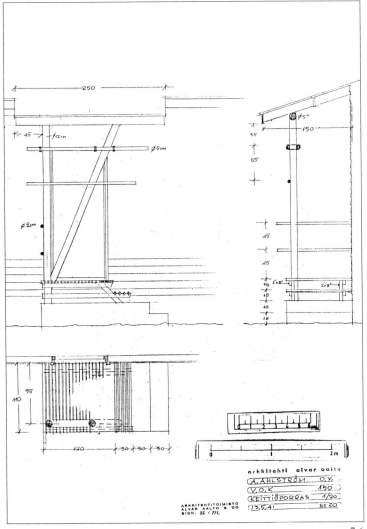

7.6

8. Experimental House, Muuratsalo / ムーラッツアロの実験住宅

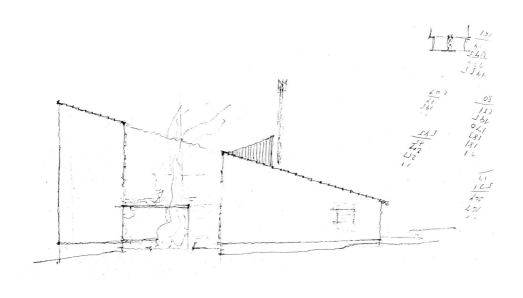

8.1

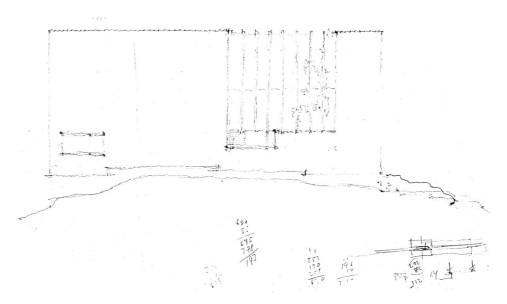

8.2

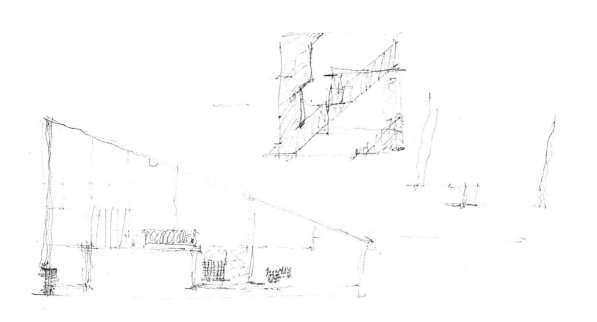

8.3

8.1, 8.2, 8.3: Sketches.
8.4: Roof plan, scale: 1/400.
8.5: Plan, scale: 1/400.
8.6: East-west section through courtyard, looking from south, scale: 1/200.
8.7: East-west section through living and studio, looking from south, scale: 1/200.
8.8: North elevation, scale: 1/200.
8.9: South-north section through bedroom, looking from east, scale: 1/200.

8.1、8.2、8.3：スケッチ。
8.4：屋根伏せ図。縮尺：1/400。
8.5：平面図。縮尺：1/400。
8.6：中庭を通る東－西断面図、南側より見る。縮尺1/200。
8.7：居間、スタジオを通る東－西断面図、南側より見る。縮尺1/200。
8.8：北立面図。縮尺1/200。
8.9：寝室を通る南－北断面図、東側より見る。縮尺：1/200。

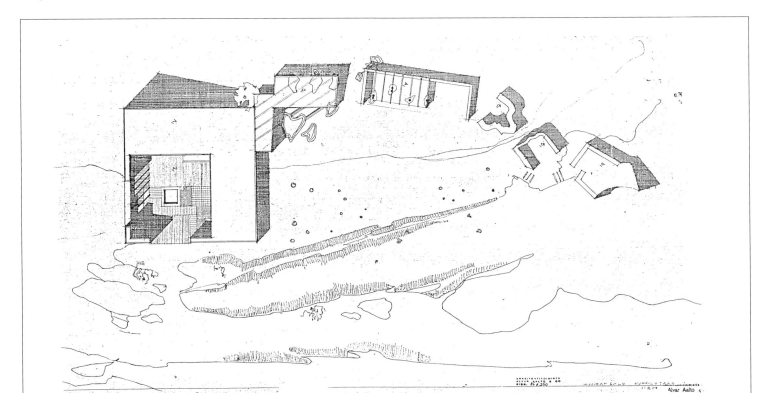

8.4

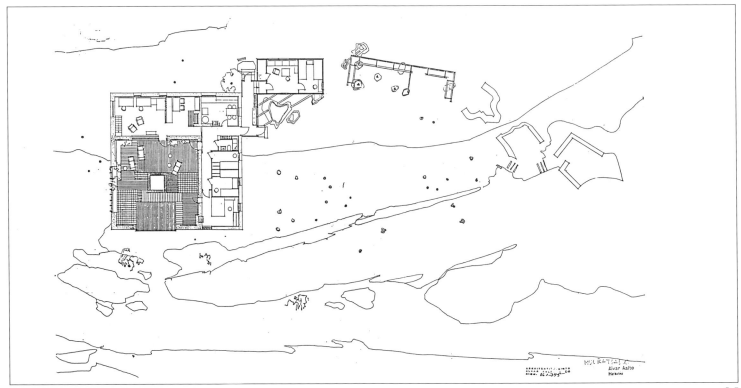

8.5

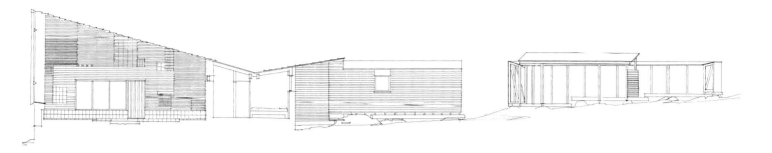

8.6

8.7

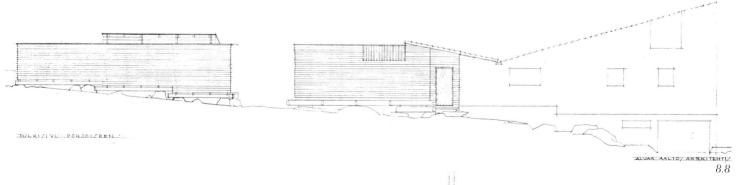

8.8

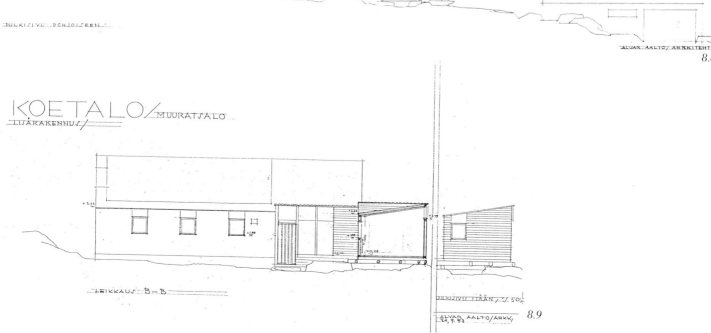

8.9

8.10, 8.11: Drawings of sauna beside the lake.

8.10、8.11：湖畔に建つサウナの図面。

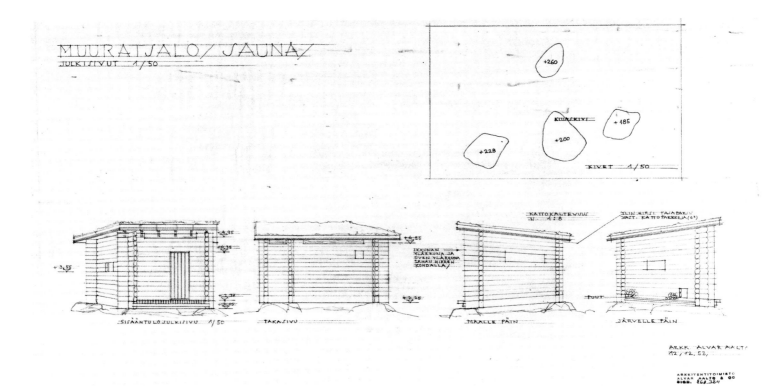

8.10

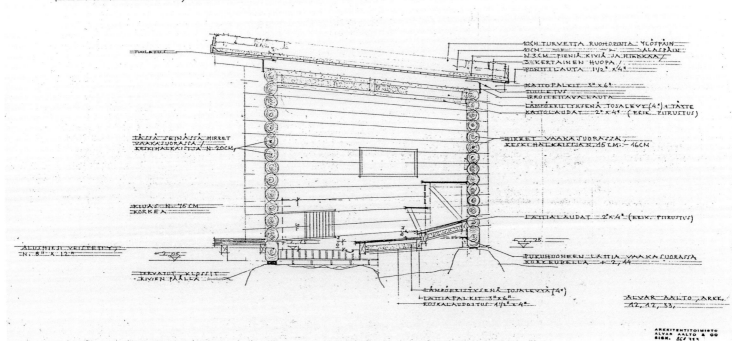

8.11

9. Maison Carré/ メゾン・カレ

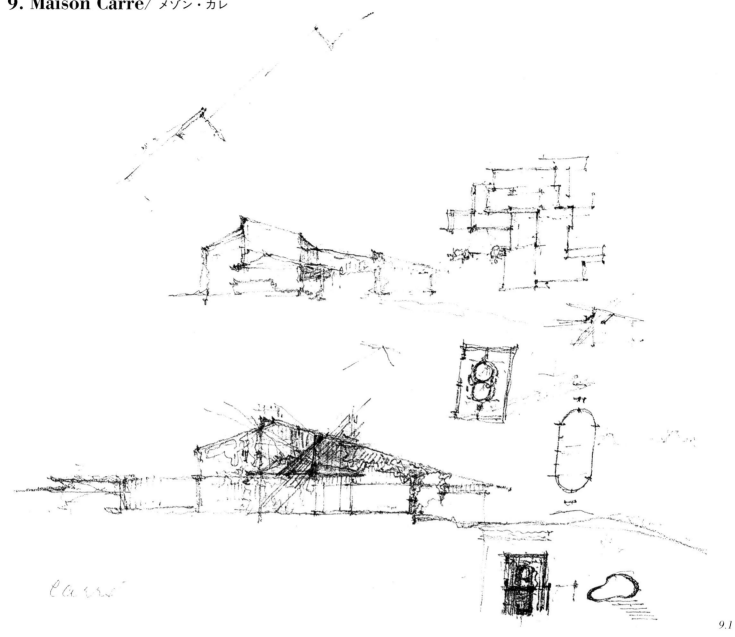

9.1

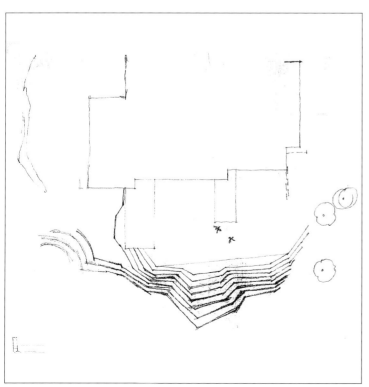

9.2

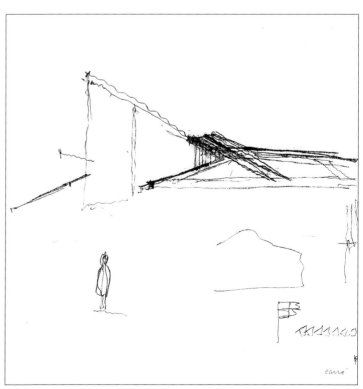

9.3

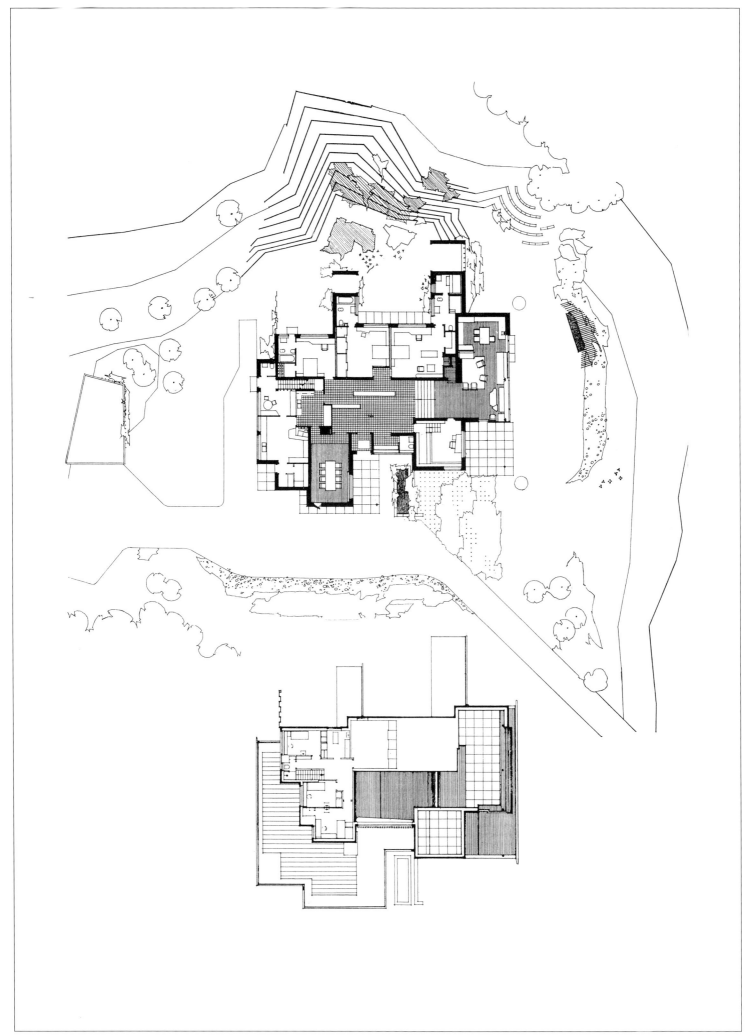

9.4

9.1, 9.2, 9.3: Sketches.
9.4: Ground floor plan and 2nd floor plan, 1/400.
9.5: Entrance side (north) elevation, scale: 1/200.
9.6: Pool side (south) elevation, scale: 1/200.
9.7: West elevation, scale: 1/200.

9.1、9.2、9.3：スケッチ。
9.4：1、2階平面図。縮尺：1/400。
9.5：エントランス側（北）立面図。縮尺：1/200。
9.6：プール側（南）立面図。縮尺：1/200。
9.7：西立面図。縮尺：1/200。

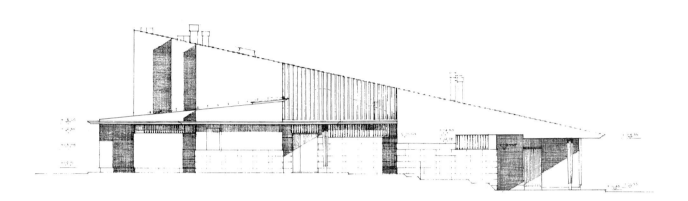

9.5

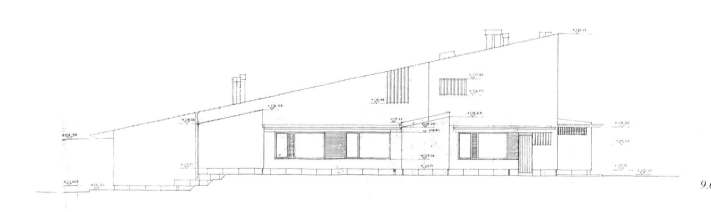

9.6

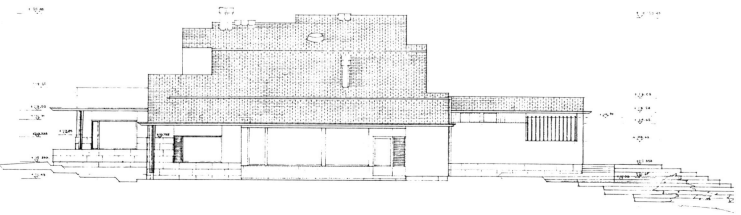

9.7

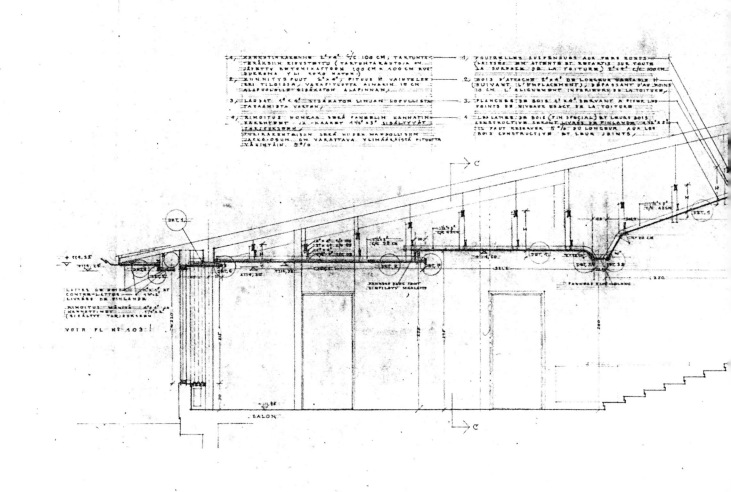

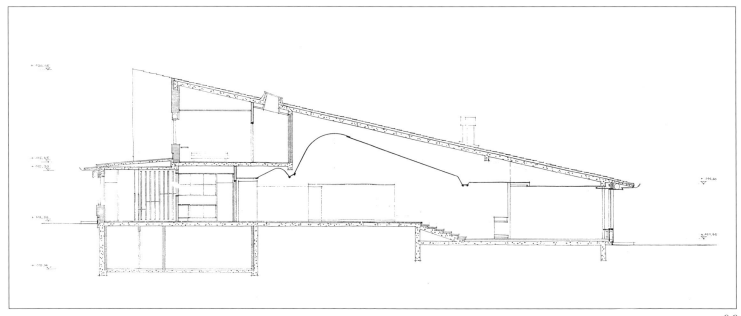

9.8: East-west section through the hall with curved ceiling.
9.9: Sectional detail through the hall.
9.10: Detail of a column.

9.8：湾曲した天井を持つホールの東―西断面図。
9.9：ホールを通る断面詳細図。
9.10：柱の詳細図。

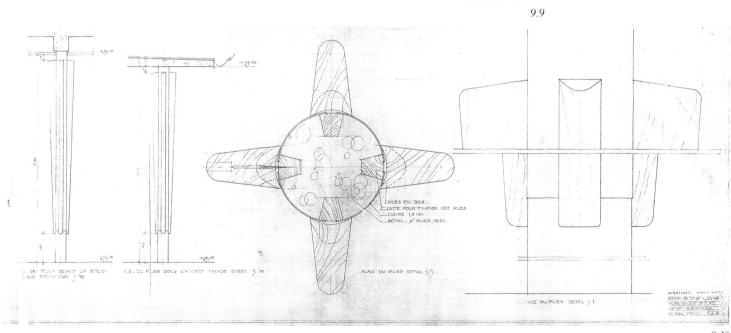

9.9

9.10

10. Manager's House B, Enso-Gutzeit / エンソ・グートツァイト社管理者の家B棟

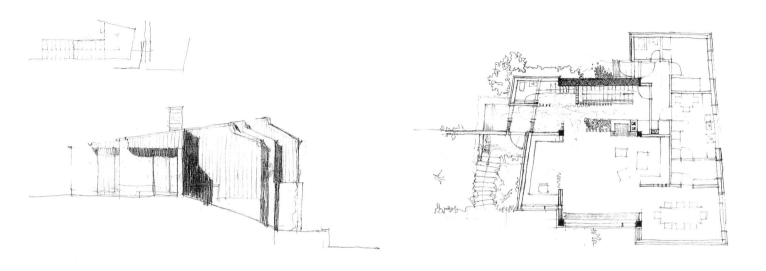

10.1　　　　　　　　　　　　　　　　　　　　10.2

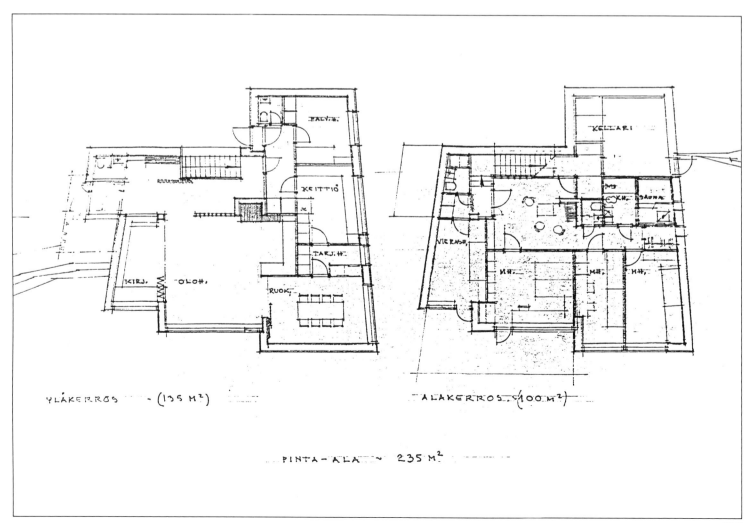

10.3

10.1, 10.2: Sketches.
10.3: Entrance floor plan (left) and upper floor plan, scale: 1/200.
10.4: East-west section, scale: 1/200.
10.5: North elevation, scale: 1/200.
10.6: South elevation, scale: 1/200.
10.7: West elevation. scale: 1/200.
10.8: East elevation, scale: 1/200.

10.1、10.2：スケッチ。
10.3：入口階と上階の平面図。縮尺：1/200。
10.4：東−西断面図。縮尺：1/200。
10.5：北立面図。縮尺：1/200。
10.6：南立面図。縮尺：1/200。
10.7：西立面図。縮尺：1/200。
10.8：東立面図。縮尺：1/200。

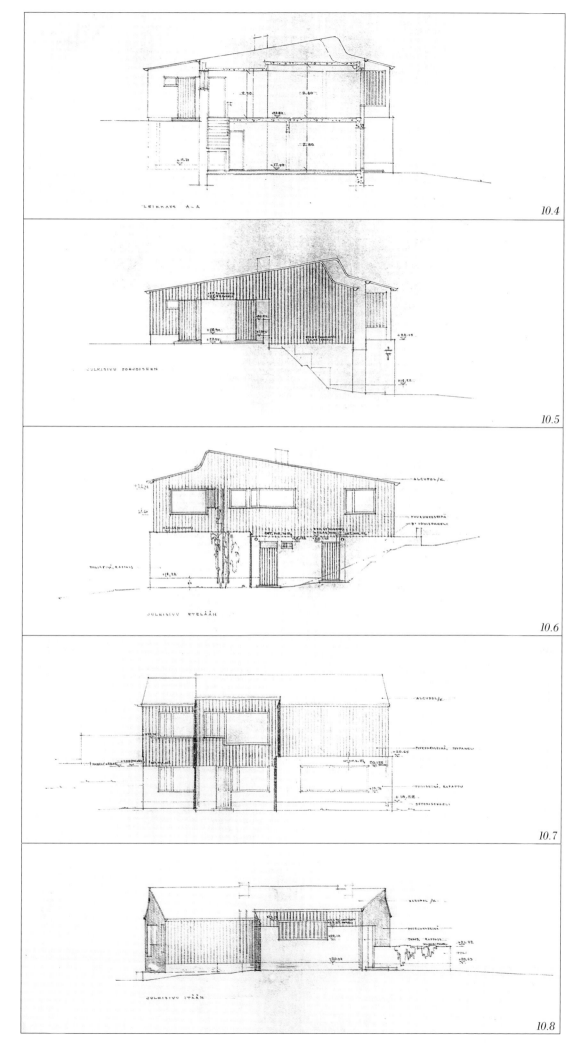

11. Manager's House C, Enso-Gutzeit / エンソ・グートツァイト社管理者の家C棟

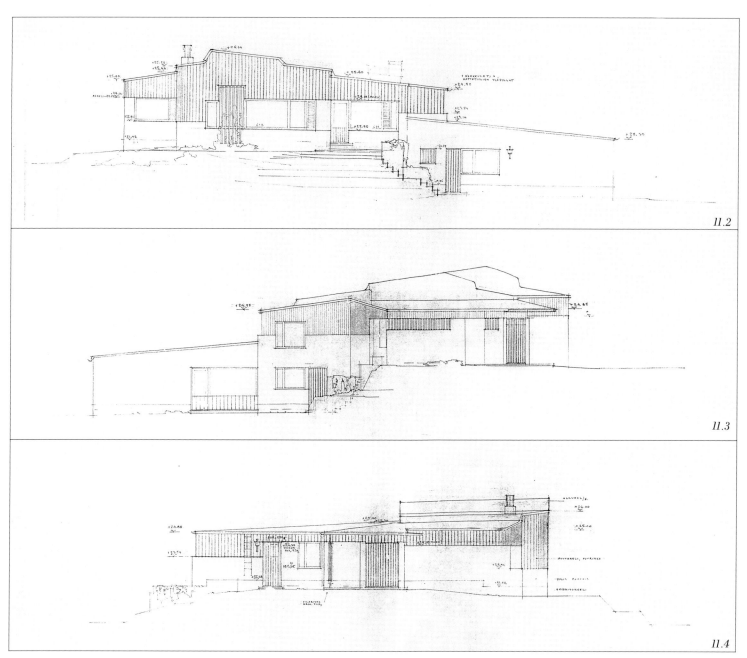

11.2

11.3

11.4

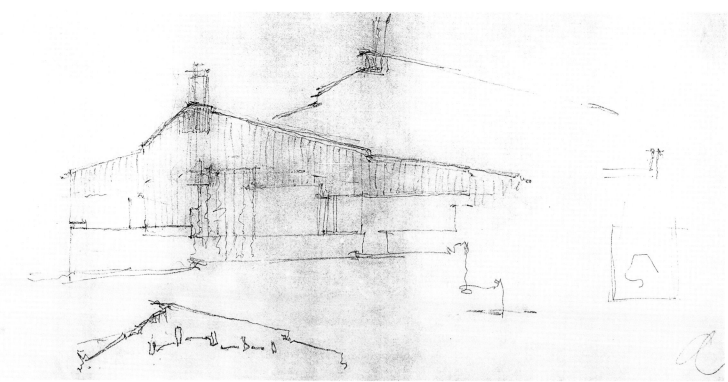

11.5

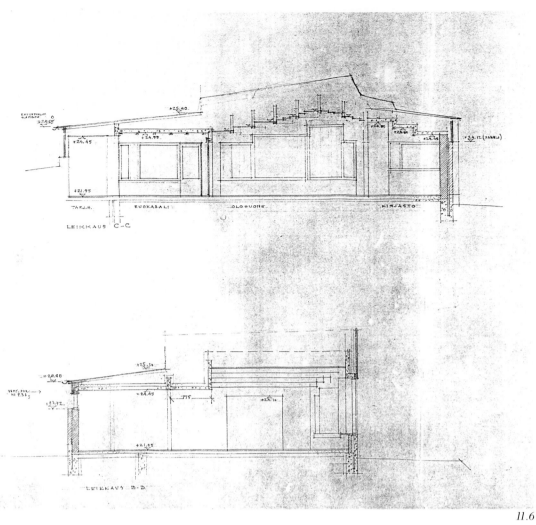

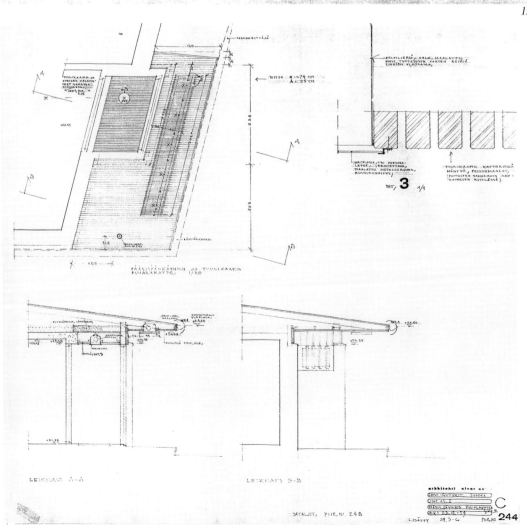

11.1: Entrance floor plan (below) and upper floor plan, scale: 1/200.
11.2: West elevation, scale: 1/200.
11.3: East elevation, scale: 1/200.
11.4: North elevation, scale: 1/200.
11.5: Sketch.
11.6: Sections through living room.
11.7: Detail drawing of gutter and lighting systems.

11.1：入口階（下）と上階の平面図。縮尺：1/200。
11.2：西立面図。縮尺：1/200。
11.3：東立面図。縮尺：1/200。
11.4：北立面図。縮尺：1/200。
11.5：スケッチ。
11.6：居間を通る断面図。
11.7：樋と照明設備の詳細図。

11.6

11.7

1961-

Maison Aho, Rovaniemi, Finland, 1964-1965

Villa Oksala, Korpilahti, Finland, 1965-1966/ 1974-1976

Villa Kokkonen, Järvenpää, Finland, 1967-1969

Villa Skeppet, Tammisaari, Finland, 1969-1970

Maison Aho
Rovaniemi, Finland 1964-1965

アホ邸
フィンランド、ロヴァニエミ　1964〜1965

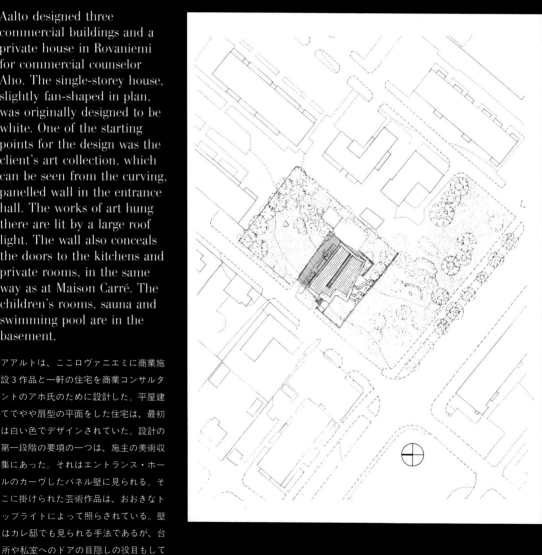

Aalto designed three commercial buildings and a private house in Rovaniemi for commercial counselor Aho. The single-storey house, slightly fan-shaped in plan, was originally designed to be white. One of the starting points for the design was the client's art collection, which can be seen from the curving, panelled wall in the entrance hall. The works of art hung there are lit by a large roof light. The wall also conceals the doors to the kitchens and private rooms, in the same way as at Maison Carré. The children's rooms, sauna and swimming pool are in the basement.

アアルトは、ここロヴァニエミに商業施設3作品と一軒の住宅を商業コンサルタントのアホ氏のために設計した。平屋建てでやや扇型の平面をした住宅は、最初は白い色でデザインされていた。設計の第一段階の要項の一つは、施主の美術収集にあった。それはエントランス・ホールのカーヴしたパネル壁に見られる。そこに掛けられた芸術作品は、おおきなトップライトによって照らされている。壁はカレ邸でも見られる手法であるが、台所や私室へのドアの目隠しの役目もしている。子供部屋、サウナ、プールは地階に設けられている。

Above: Site plan, scale: 1/1500.
Opposite: Front (northwest) elevation.

pp.168-169: Southwest elevation.
Opposite: Entrance hall.
Above: View behind panel wall towards the kitchen.

p168〜169：南西立面。左頁：エントランス・ホール。上：パネル壁の裏、台所の方を見る。

Above: Living room.
Opposite: Living room corner.

上：居間。右頁：居間のコーナー部分。

Alvar Aalto designed a summer home for his friend Päivö Oksala, a classics professor, on an island in Lake Päijänne, 30 kilometres to the south of Muuratsalo. The villa has a fan-shaped plan with a distinct separation between private spaces and 'public'. The whole of the south wall of the large living room is window. A special characteristic of the exterior architecture is the natural stone plinth.

ムーラッツァロ島から南へ30km、パイヤン湖に浮かぶ小島に、アアルトは友人で古典の教授であるパイヴォ・オクサラ氏の別荘を設計した。この住宅は、公私の空間が明らかに分けられた扇形の平面形をしている。大きな居間の南面の壁はほとんどが窓になっている。建築的に特筆すべきは、外部の自然石を使用した台座である。

Right: Site plan, scale: 1/800.
Opposite: View of Villa Oksala on Ruotsola Island.

右：配置図。縮尺：1/800。右頁：ルオッツォラ島にあるオクサラ邸。

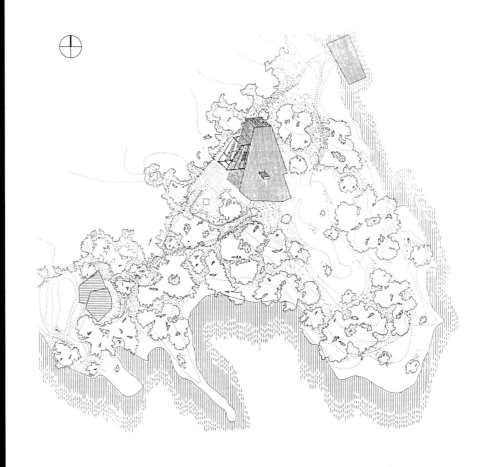

Above: Front (west) elevation.
Opposite: South elevation.

上：玄関側（西）立面。右頁：南立面。

Above and opposite: Views of living room.

上、左頁：居間。

Alvar Aalto's friend the composer and academician Joonas Kokkonen commissioned the drawings for his house in 1967. Developed from outline sketches made on a restaurant tablecloth, the house is hidden away in its natural surroundings almost without a facade at all, but inside is like a beautiful, wooden musical-box. The wooden-built house is linked to the log sauna and the swimming pool by a pergola along the slope. (See text on p.12)

アアルトの友人で作曲家・アカデミー会員のヨナス・コッコネン氏は、1967年、自邸のドローイングを依頼した。レストランのテーブルクロスの上で描かれたスケッチから発展して、この住宅は自然の周囲環境に隠されて、ほとんどファサードがなくなっている。しかし、内部は美しく木でつくられたオルゴールのようである。この木造住宅は、坂道に沿ったパーゴラによって丸太づくりのサウナとプールに連結されている。(詳しくは論文21頁参照)

Right: Site plan, scale: 1/800.
Opposite: Canopy of the entrance (see drawing 14.6).

右:配置図。縮尺:1/800。右頁:玄関のキャノピー(図14.6参照)。

pp.182-183: View of the garden and the pergola from the west.
Opposite: View of workroom with canvas canopy (see drawing 14.8).
Above: Fireplace in the living room.

182〜183頁：庭とパーゴラを西から見る。左頁：キャンヴァス・キャノピー（図14.8参照）が吊されている仕事部屋。上：居間の断炉。

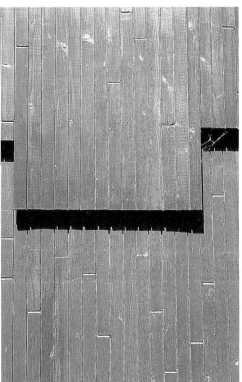

Above: Details. Clockwise from top left: Lanterns from a skylight, lamp, exterior wall, wall-to-floor joint. Opposite: Detail of lamp and fireplace chimney.

左頁：ディテール。左上から時間回り：スカイライトから吊されている照明、照明、外壁、壁と床のジョイント。上：照明器具と断炉の煙突のディテール。

Alvar Aalto designed for his friend and biographer Göran Schildt "a house that would keep him in Finland." The Villa Skeppet is in parklike surroundings beside the sea. This differs from Aalto's other one-family houses in that the freely flowing space works vertically here, from the entrance hall to the living room on the upper floor. (See text on p.12)

アアルトの伝記執筆者で友人のヨーラン・シルツのために、アアルトは「彼をフィンランドに留めるための家」を設計した。このシルツ邸は、海沿いの公園のような周辺環境の中にある。この作品は、他のアアルトの住宅作品と異なり、自由に流れるような空間が垂直方向に、エントランス・ホールから二階の居間まで広がっている。(詳しくは論文21頁参照)

Right: Site plan, scale: 1/800.
Opposite: Front (west) elevation.

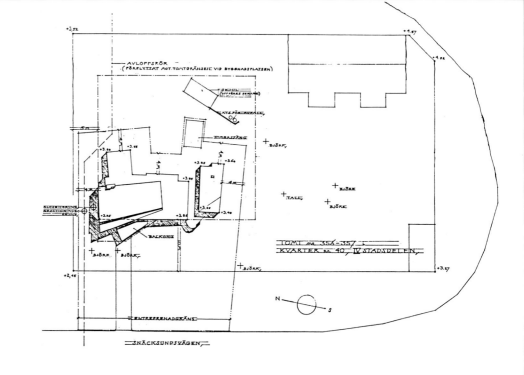

pp.190–191: View of front (west) elevation. Opposite: View from the south. Above: View of living room, facing west. pp.194–195: View of living room, facing north. p.196: View up the stairs to the living room.

190〜191頁：玄関側（西）立面。左頁：南から見る。上：居間の西側を見る。194〜195頁：居間の北側を見る。196頁：居間へと続く階段を見上げる。

12. Maison Aho / アホ邸

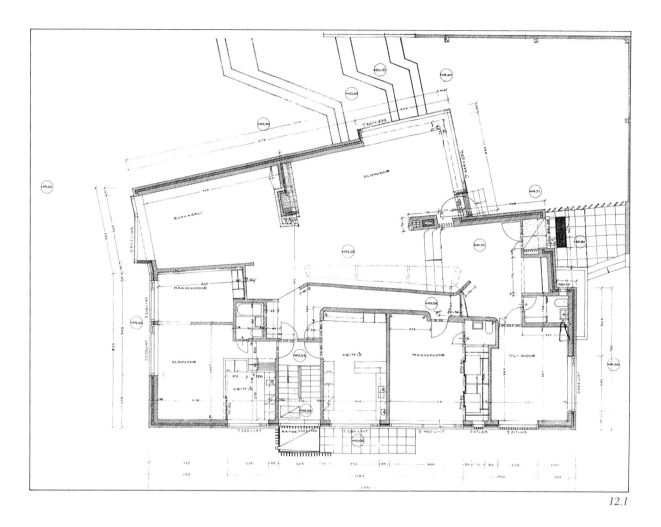

12.1

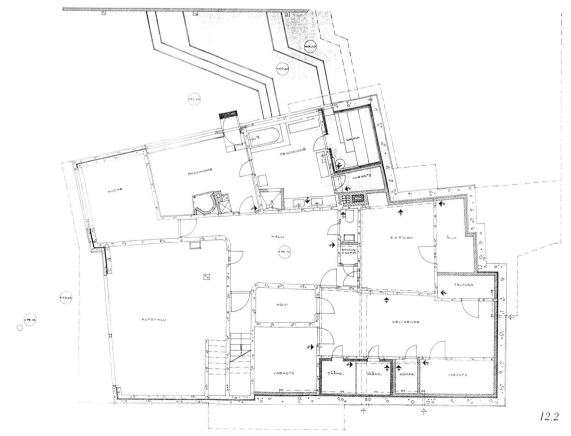

12.2

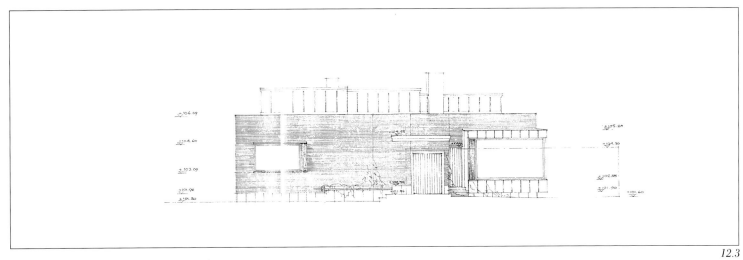

12.3

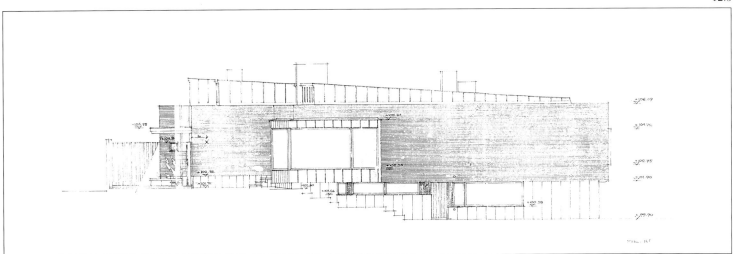

12.4

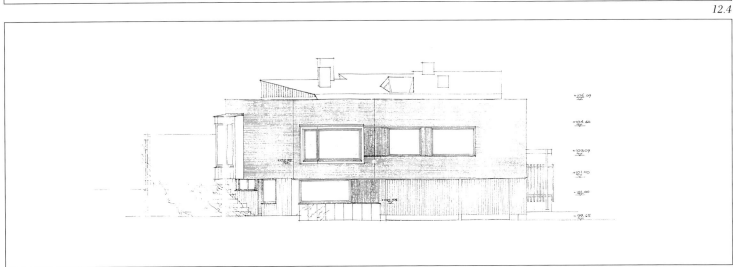

12.5

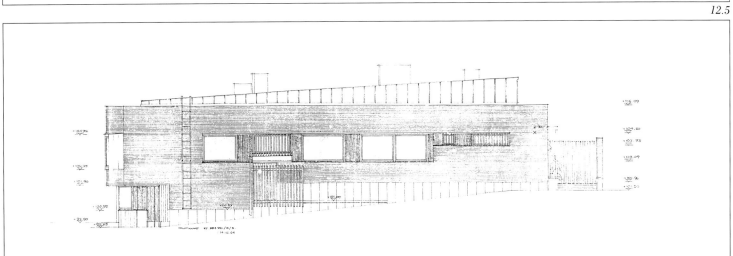

12.6

12.1: Entrance floor plan, scale: 1/200.
12.2: Basement floor plan, scale: 1/200.
12.3: Northwest elevation, scale: 1/200.
12.4: Southwest elevation, scale: 1/200.
12.5: Southeast elevation, scale: 1/200.
12.6: Northeast elevation, scale: 1/200.
12.7: Section.
12.8: Roof sections, scale: 1/80.
12.9: Detailed elevation and plan of window, scale: 1/60. Detail of joint, scale: 1/3.
12.10: Brass flagpole, scale: 1/75. Plan and elevation, scale: 1/3.

12.1：エントランス階平面図。縮尺：1/200。
12.2：地階平面図。縮尺：1/200。
12.3：北西立面図。縮尺：1/200。
12.4：南西立面図。縮尺：1/200。
12.5：南東立面図。縮尺：1/200。
12.6：北東立面図。縮尺：1/200。
12.7：断面図。
12.8：屋根断面図。縮尺：1/80。
12.9：窓詳細図。縮尺：1/60。接続部分詳細図。縮尺：1/3。
12.10：真鍮製の旗竿、全体図。縮尺：1/75。平面と立面図。縮尺：1/3。

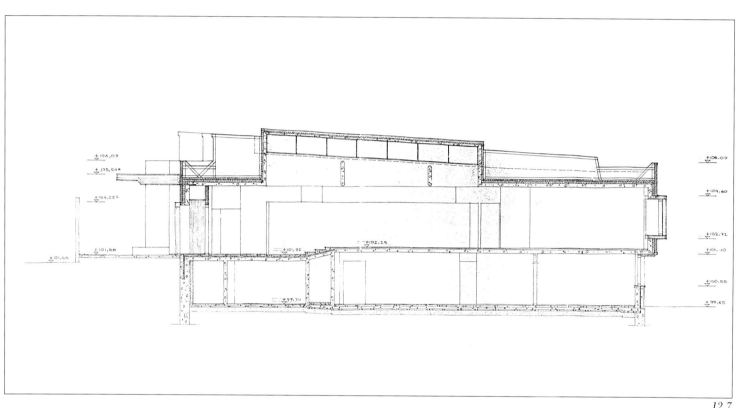

12.7

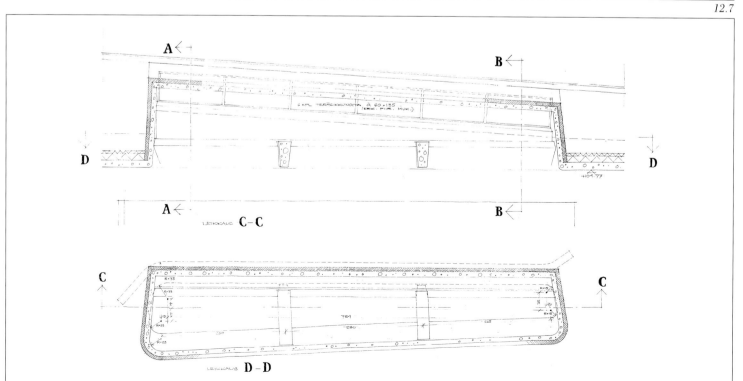

12.8

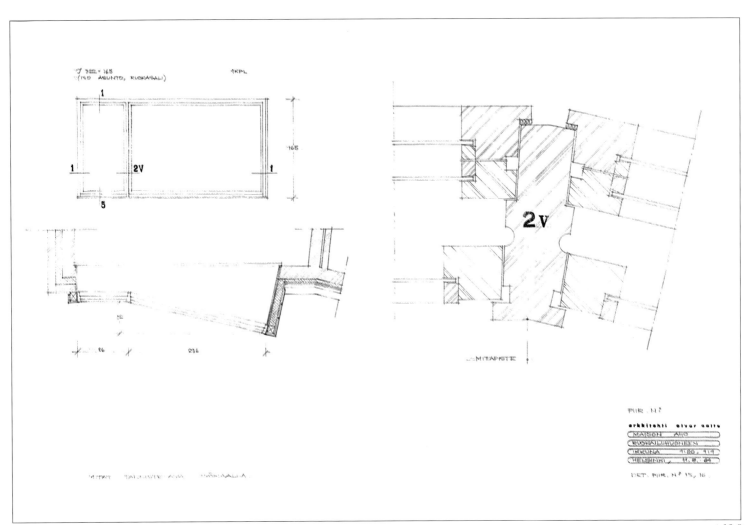

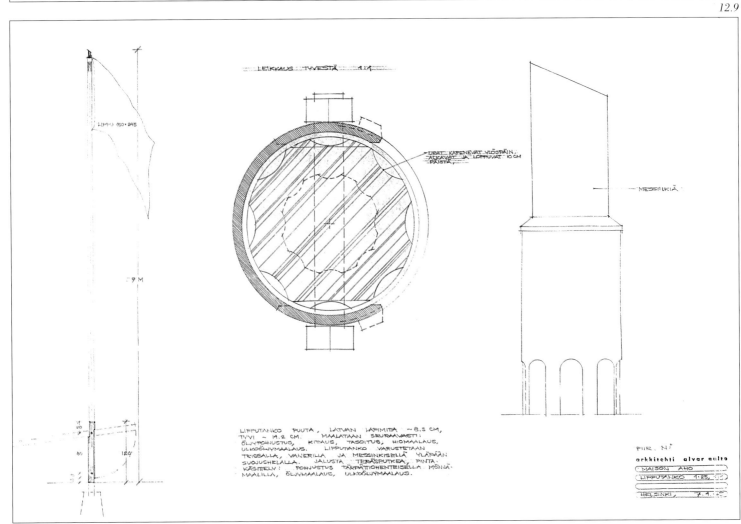

13. Villa Oksala / オクサラ邸別荘

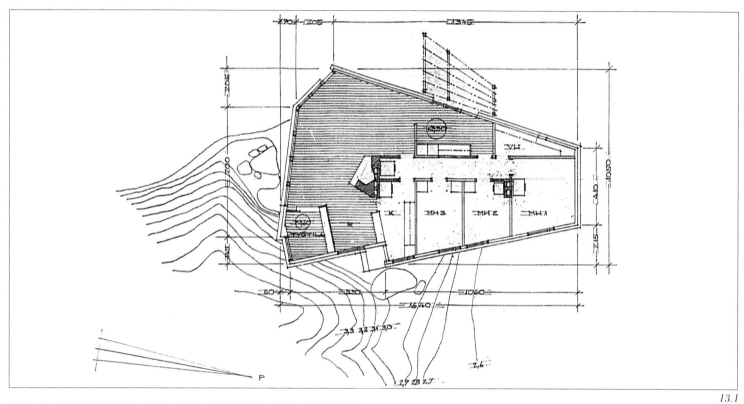

13.1

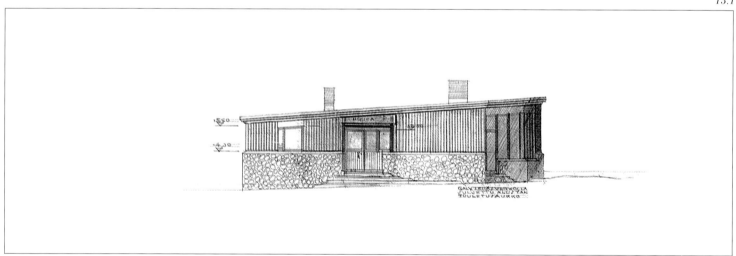

13.2

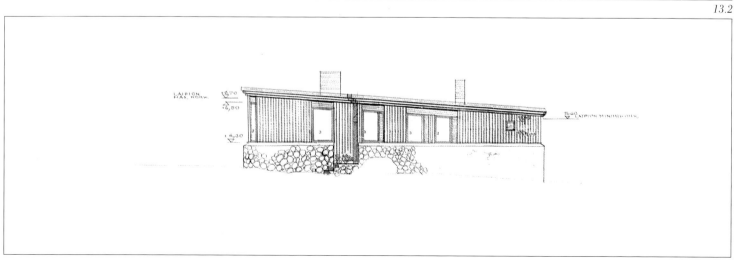

13.3

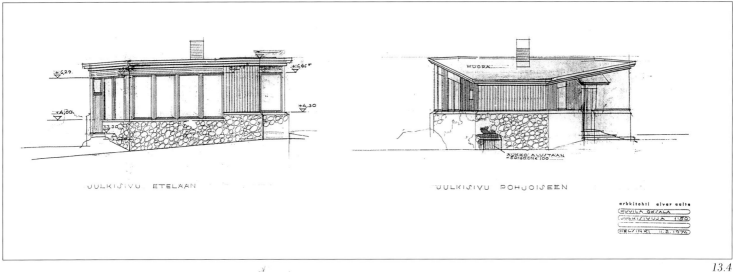

13.4

13.1: Plan, scale: 1/200.
13.2: West elevation, scale: 1/200.
13.3: East elevation, scale: 1/200.
13.4: South and north elevations, scale: 1/200.
13.5: Sauna. Plan, section, south elevation, north elevation, and east elevation, scale: 1/200.
13.6: Short section, longitudinal section, scale: 1/100.
13.7: Sections and plans of the entrance canopy, scale: 1/100. Details, scale: 1/25.

13.1：平面図。縮尺：1/200。
13.2：西立面図。縮尺：1/200。
13.3：東立面図。縮尺：1/200。
13.4：南と北立面図。縮尺：1/200。
13.5：サウナ。平面図、断面図、南立面図、北立面図、東立面図。縮尺：1/200。
13.6：短手断面図。長手断面図。
13.7：エントランス・キャノピーの断面と平面図。縮尺：1/100。詳細図。縮尺：1/25。

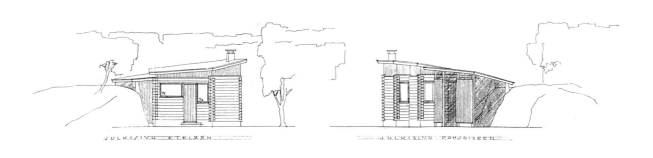

13.5

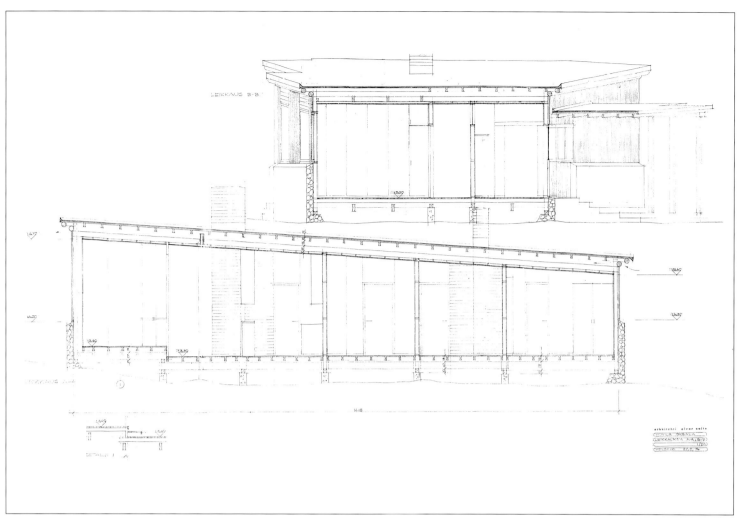

13.6

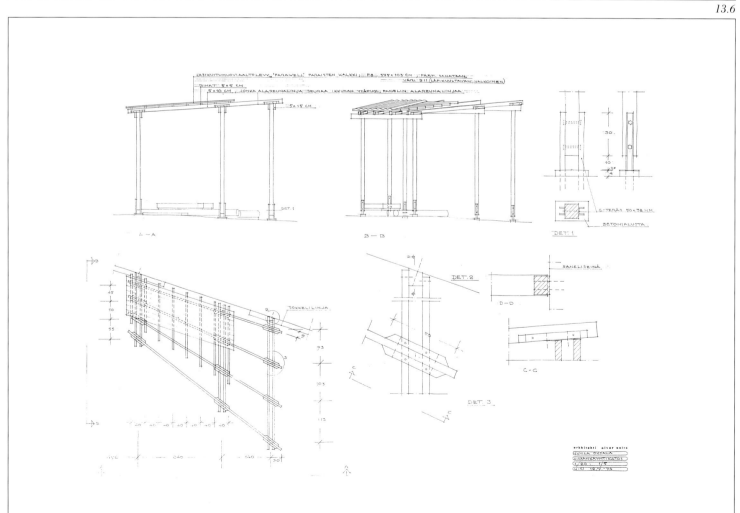

13.7

14. Villa Kokkonen / コッコネン邸

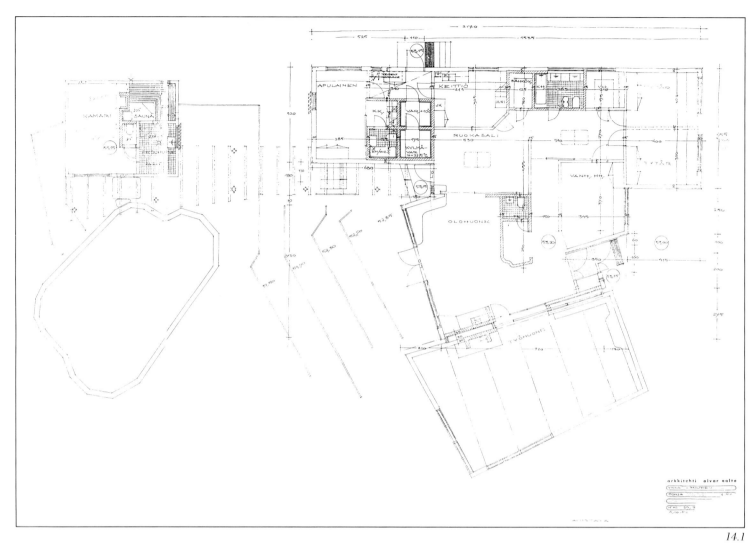

14.1

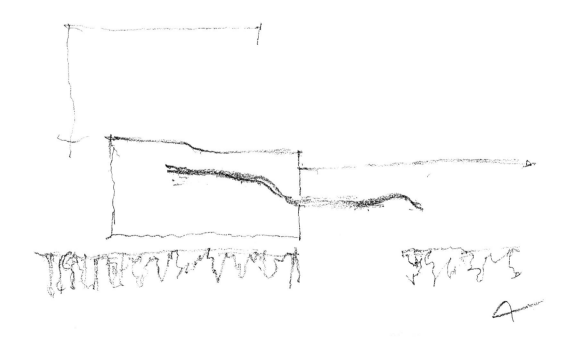

14.2

14.1: Plan, scale: 1/200.
14.2: Sketch of the entrance facade.
14.3: South elevation, scale: 1/200.
14.4: East elevation, scale: 1/200.
14.5: Sketch of the south elevation.

14.1：平面図。縮尺：1/200。
14.2：玄関ファサードのスケッチ。
14.3：南立面図。縮尺：1/200。
14.4：東立面図。縮尺：1/200。
14.5：南立面のスケッチ。

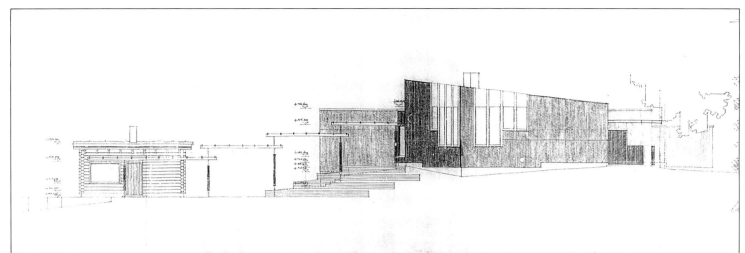

14.3

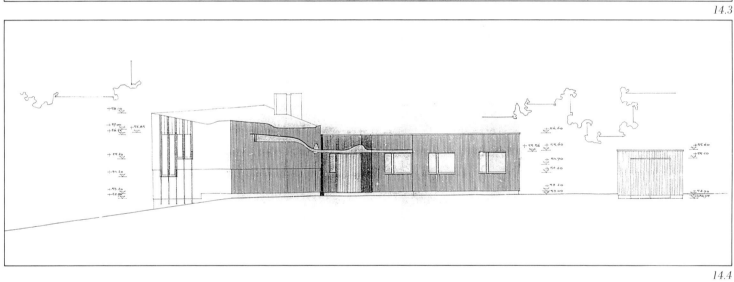

14.4

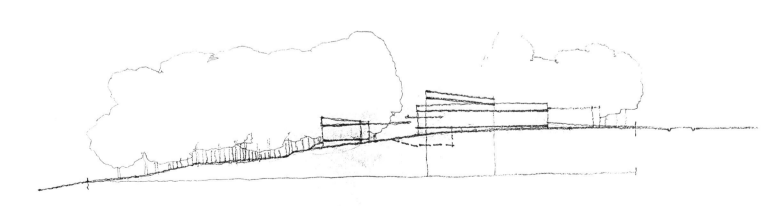

14.5

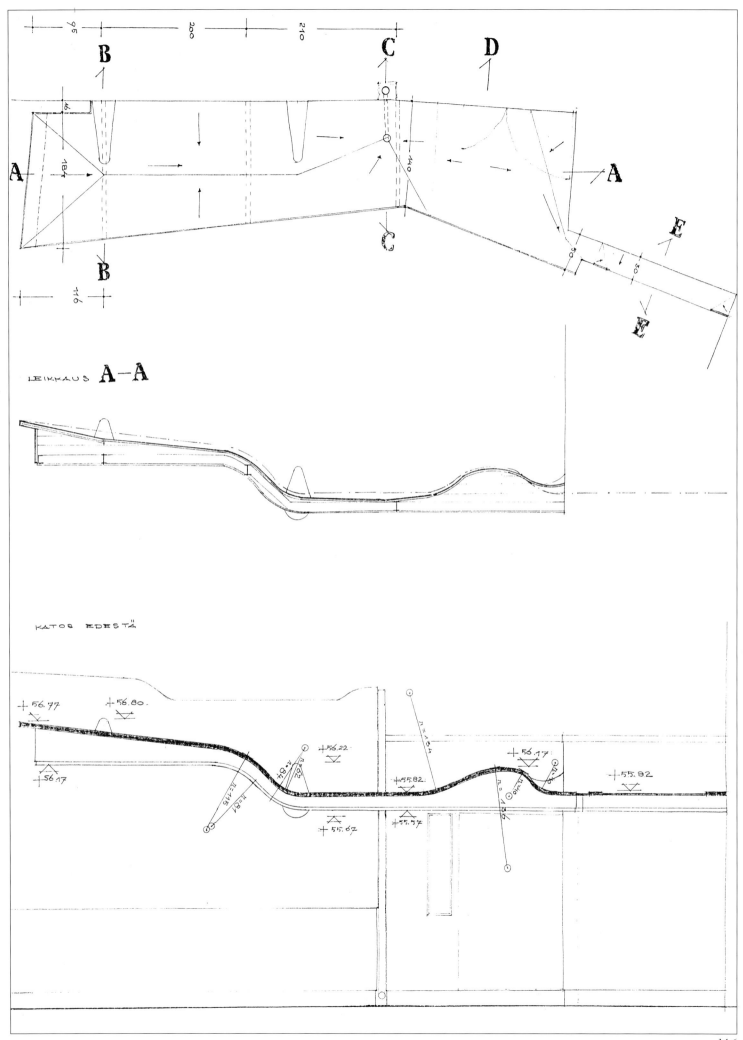

LEIKKAUS A-A

KATOS EDESTÄ

14.6: Roof plan and sections, scale: 1/50.
14.7: Fireplace. Section, elevation, and perspective.
14.8: Working room canopy. Plan and section, scale: 1/100. Detail of attachment, scale: 1/5.

14.6：キャノピーの屋根伏図と断面図。縮尺：1/50。
14.7：断炉。断面図、立面図、パース。
14.8：仕事部屋キャノピー。縮尺：1/100。接続部分詳細。縮尺：1/5。

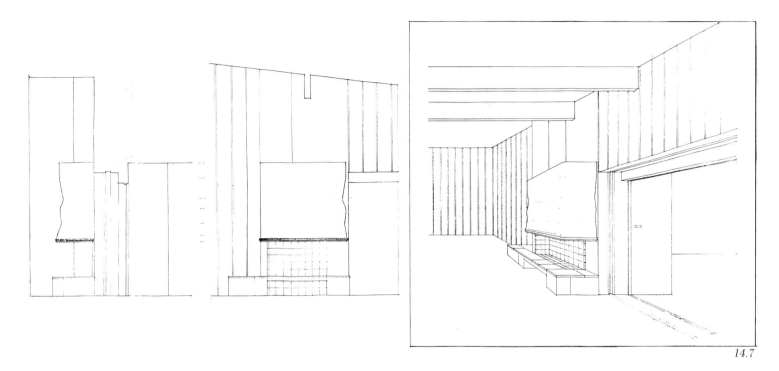

14.7

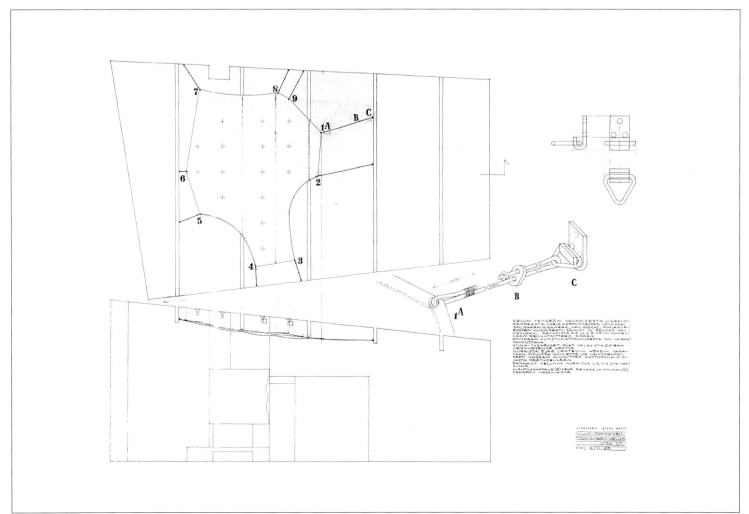

14.8

15. Villa Skeppet / シルツ邸

15.1: 2nd floor plan, ground floor plan, scale: 1/200.
15.2: West and south facades.
15.3: East and north facades.
15.4: Short sections.
15.5: Longitudinal sections.
15.6: Fireplace.
15.7: Window. Plan and elevation, scale: 1/200. Details, scale: 1/10.
15.8: Fence. Plan and elevation.
15.9: Fireplace chimney. Elevation and plan.
15.10: Oil painting. A gift from Aalto to Göran Schildt.

15.1：2階平面図、1階平面図。縮尺：1/200。
15.2：西と南立面図。
15.3：東と北立面図。
15.4：短手断面図。
15.5：長手断面図。
15.6：断炉。
15.7：窓。平面と立面図。縮尺：1/200。詳細図。縮尺：1/10。
15.8：フェンス。平面と立面図。
15.9：断炉の煙突。立面と平面図。
15.10：油絵。アアルトからヨーラン・シルツへの贈り物。

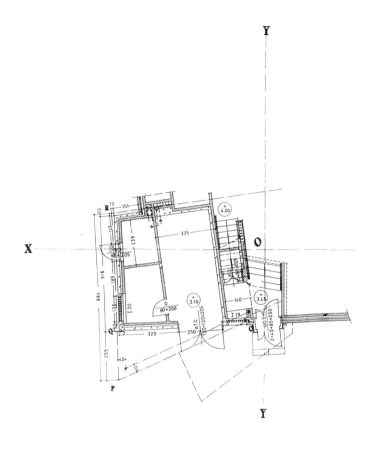

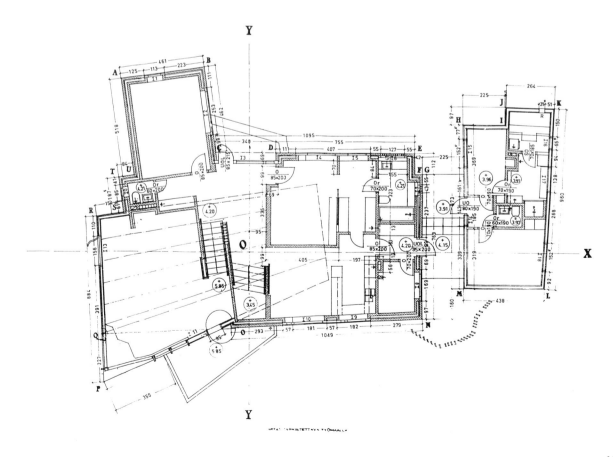

15.1

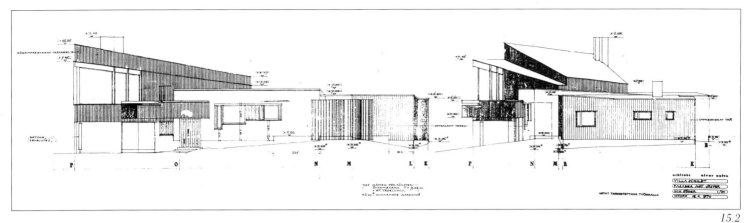

15.2

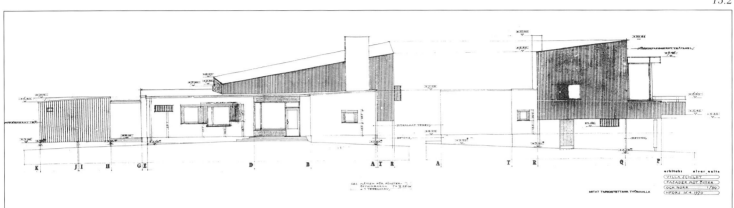

15.3

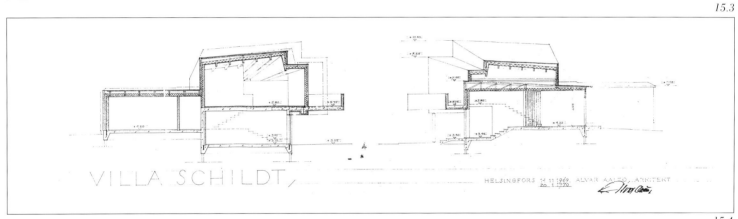

15.4

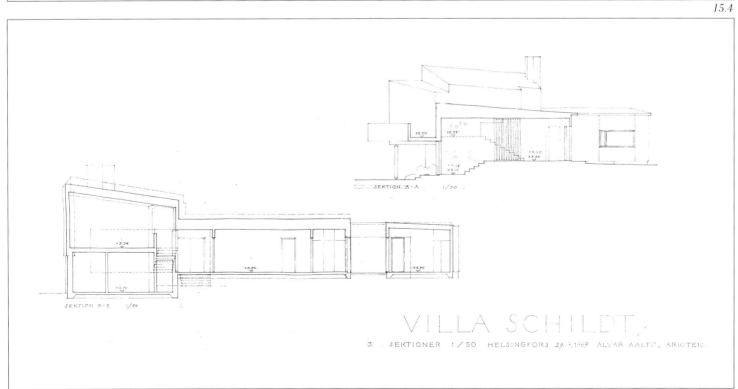

15.5

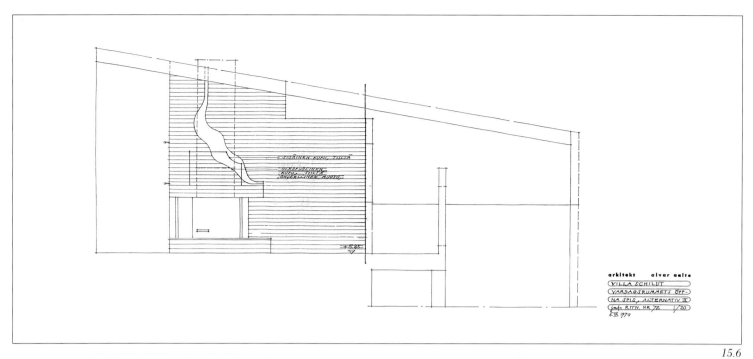

15.6

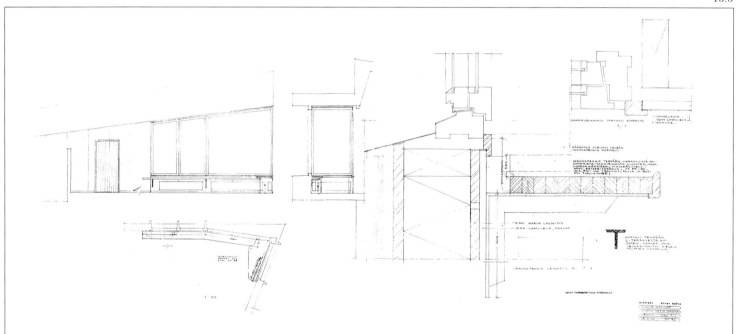

15.7

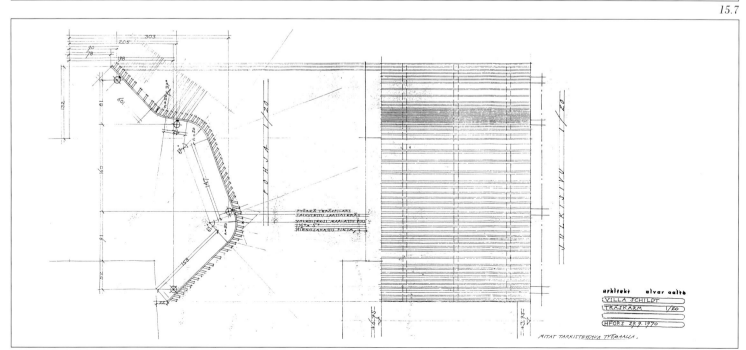

15.8

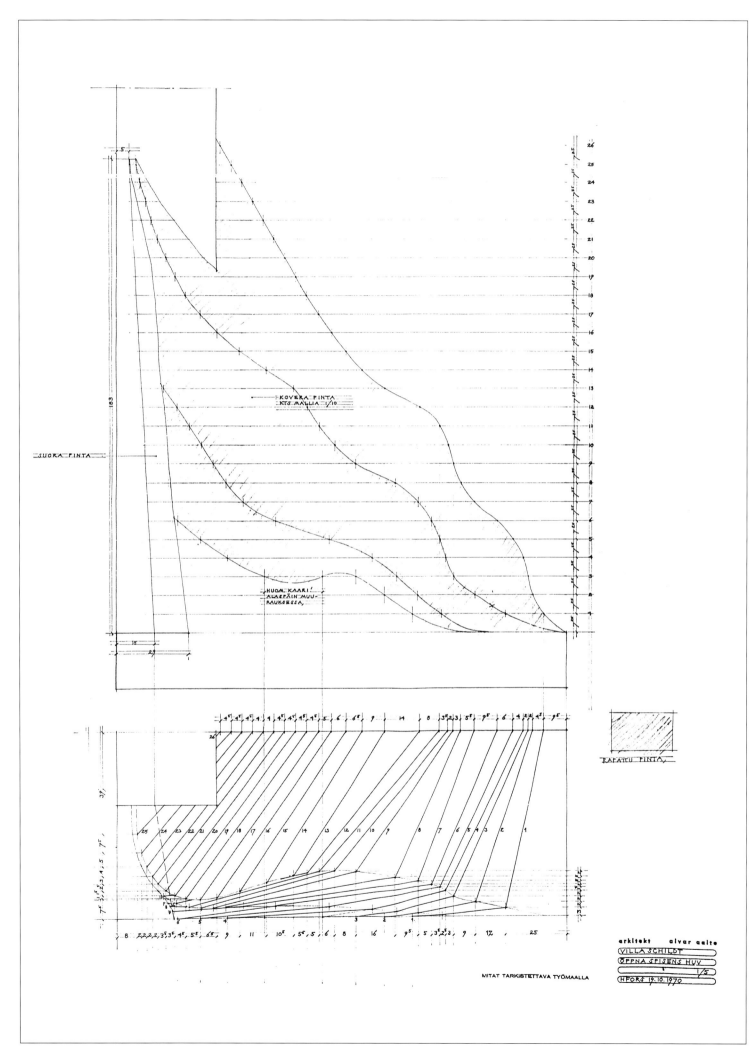

15.10

Visiting the Houses of Aalto
Matti Sanaksenaho

アアルトの住宅を訪ねて
マッティ・サナクセンアホ
土居純訳

"I build" went the memorable motto of Alvar Aalto, the architect. He was a man of prodigious industry, realising over 300 buildings during his long career. The range was wide, from small summer cottages to grand public buildings, from doorknobs to urban designs.

Today, Alvar Aalto also refers to a myriad of stories, studies, books and publications. His name is honoured by a medal, a commemorative coin, and a symposium. The Finnish 50-mark banknote carries the image of the Finlandia Hall on one side; on the other, there is the portrait of the architect, glancing up at the sky. It is difficult to approach Aalto with the objectivity every architect should be approached with; it is equally difficult to adopt the necessary subjectivity, the only way to enter the realm of a given building. When it comes to Aalto, this realm only too often seems preconceived, like a heavily dogmatised religion which only gives answers, leaving no room for questions or discovery.

For the contemporary generation of young architects Aalto is not a contemporary. Our image of him is neither personal nor complete, it consists of small particles. It is difficult to analyse the work of the late architect by a careful study of the flow of information available, of everything that has been said and written. The essence of architecture often succumbs to the media circus. It is impossible to objectively approach something that has been presented a thousand times through various media. Moreover, the image of Aalto is focused around his personality. This is understandable; Aalto seems to have been a charismatic man. He must also have been fully aware of the general tendency to mix a person and his achievements. As an old man, he once gave this piece of advice to his biographer: "Write about architectural problems, not mine."

"I build" is a key to the true essence of the architect's work. The existing buildings provide an unfeigned document on Aalto's achievements. The world has changed and the young generation have the possibility to travel; there are ships and trains and airplanes. The best way to acquaint oneself with architecture is not to read about it: it is to look, touch, smell and listen to it—a building only gains meaning when it becomes part of human life. This piece of writing presents one such journey, a personal trip to visit Alvar Aalto's houses.

Airborne

Looking from the sky, the Finnish landscape is tangible enough. A green carpet of forests is sectioned by blue, beautifully winding lakes and rivers. The roads follow the contour of the land, looking like opened streamers. But it is the shoreline which draws the most refined shapes; a continuous, soft shape moulded by water in the course of time. The villages are visible as small groups of buildings usually located along roads, rivers, and lakes. Sometimes I can spot a church, rising above the other buildings in the middle of the village. Towns and cities are surprisingly scarce, compared to the amount of woodland and water. Viewed from the airplane, the landscape does not reveal the problems and failures that yet are the reality. Finland has environmental problems just like continental Europe, and the protection of nature is often endangered. But when I look at the landscape from the plane window, it has originality and beauty. I order a coffee and a calvados, now looking back on the events of last week.

Dining Out in Helsinki

Our journey begins with a night at the Savoy, the restaurant designed by Alvar Aalto. We have just completed an extensive competition entry and got it mailed in time. Competitions are a strong tradition among Finnish architects, as are the wrapping-up parties afterwards. Mie, our friend from Japan, has just arrived from Tokyo and joins us. When we enter the restaurant, it is practically empty; at the corner table there is a group of businessmen chatting over coffee and cognac. The most powerful impression of the space is the lights of the wintery city, revealing an alternative view of Helsinki. The large glass surfaces open up views in all directions. The Savoy is one of the rare places offering a view over the horizon of the city. The interior is elegant, clad with wood. The relationship between the wooden surfaces and the landscape is what makes the restaurant both distinguished and continental as well as cosy, and the lobby is pleasant. The restaurant appears a good example of successful cooperation between the architect and the client. In fact, a good building requires not only a good architect but also a good client and a good builder. Ahlström Ltd., which ordered the Savoy, was a perfect example. The plywood surfaces of the ceiling and the walls are reminiscent of the Finnish forest industry, of which Ahlström was and still is a part.

The menu seems to have remained practically unchanged. We order vodka with berry liqueur for aperitif, some bottles of beer, and ice water. The waiter seems to be fully aware of the traditions and esteem of the place. For starters, we are having rawpickled salmon and whitefish to honour our Japanese friend, an ardent angler and a fan of raw fish.

With the conversation really getting under way, the atmosphere becomes more intense and even the space appears smaller. The lighting is directed straight at the table with a lamp hanging low. Through the well-formed dome, the light contributes to the intense atmosphere around the table. The other tables and the rest of the restaurant seem to disappear, and what remains is your own table and friends. Thanks to the lighting, we all participate actively in the conversation despite the fact that there are eight of us. We choose vorschmack for the main course, thus paying tribute to Marshal Mannerheim, who according to legend was a regular customer here. After finishing our meal, we linger for a few hours more, sipping brandy and enjoying the silence of the empty restaurant. One of us relates to us an anecdote of Aalto.

The planning meeting for the Otaniemi campus, which Aalto was later to realise, was held at the Savoy. Aalto was a candidate for chief designer. The meeting developed into a terrible row, ending as a full-fledged fight. One of Aalto's assistants bit the client in the ankle, shouting: "Honour architecture and give the job to Aalto!"

We pay the bill. A coherent interior is an unusual sight at restaurants nowadays. It is often rock stars and specialist foreign chains who are given the assignment. As for us, we have now had our first encounter with Aalto the architect.

Introduction to Red Brick
The Finnish farmland is beautiful when frozen. The light of the autumn morning is scarce, yet sufficient to reveal the delicate nuances of nature, the soft colours. In the meagre light, the profile of the landscape is reduced to a holistical, plastic movement, which is interesting to follow through the car window. The first freezing nights have arrived and the fields are covered with a veil of frost. There are three of us on this journey. Jari drives carefully with Mie seated beside him, while I monitor the situation from the back seat. The road is slippery and we have summer tyres. But we drive at a leisurely pace; we have all the time in the world.
Jyväskylä is our first destination. Before that, we stop at Hämeenlinna, where we have a cup of coffee at the mediaeval castle. As it is a working day, all other visitors are pensioners on a coach tour. We sneak into a guided tour presenting the exhibition on the Middle Ages and admire the brickwork of the castle. The brick walls are architecture at its finest. In those days they did not attend to trivial details: they made beautiful buildings with common sense, following the local tradition famous for its unhurried mentality. The wall starts off from the ground as a construction of huge stones, continuing with smaller stones, and finally ending with small bricks in the upper parts. Lifting stones like that must have required a lot of work; this is probably why the material is lighter on the upper levels. The castle walls slant and bulge gently. The floors are everywhere slightly sloping. The long history of the touch of the human hand is omnipresent.
Jari shows us the small chapel. It is a room of some 10 × 10 metres in size, made of stone, with windows, benches, and an altar. Natural light is abundant and the general impression is beautiful, yet modest. Hämeenlinna is a good introduction to brick architecture. We choose brick as today's theme, and continue towards Jyväskylä and Aalto's brick buildings.

At the Summer Cottage
With its white patinated exterior, the redbrick building proudly rises from the Finnish lake landscape. At the same time, it blends into the landscape, revealing itself only partially when viewed from a distance. The house in Muuratsalo, the architect's summer cottage, plays with contrasts. The first gesture is grand, even pompous. It crystallises around the high-rising living room/studio and the corner gate of the inner courtyard. In contrast, what follows is a revelation of small features and details, making the whole balanced and interesting. The composition resembles a script where first something shocking is said and then the situation is calmed down with something soothing and comforting. It is this feature that makes the Muuratsalo house simultaneously deeply human and highly impressive.
We have to remember that we are dealing with a summer cottage here, something very dear to a Finn, something traditional. For a Finn, his summer cottage is where he is able to realise his innermost desire to be as one with nature. In its own special way, Muuratsalo acknowledges this devotion. From the lake, the building is approached by boat. First comes the introduction—the water, the rolling forest and the waves lapping on the round pebbles. From the shore you ascend towards the house, slipping between the trees and the stones. It feels like a ceremony. The inner courtyard serves as a gate to the building. The architect wanted to enter his cottage through antiquity. The various brick bonds and tile experiments tell us about a resident who sailed the seven seas and saw a lot, but they also bring to mind the regular summer cottage DIY pastime familiar to almost every Finn. The high corner in the side of the inner courtyard has no function whatsoever. Actually, it blocks the view to the lake. I can tell you a story about it.

The mason and Aalto start work. "Get started, and don't stop until I tell you to," says Aalto to the mason, uncorking a bottle of Koskenkorva vodka and sitting down on a stub. After finishing a second bottle, he dozes off. When the architect wakes up, the mason has got quite far, right up to the present level. Aalto springs up, shouting: "My good man, you're a genius!"

On the lakeside wall there is an opening through which you can spot the tower of Muurame church. After all, perhaps the house is not looking at the long lake landscape in the west, but instead at the southern view, to the narrow, winding sound whose ancient shape surprisingly resembles the shape of the Savoy vase so dear to the architect. The living room is situated

Finnish farmland.
フィンランドの農地。

at the end of this spatial series—or at the beginning—providing a view through the large glass window to the inner courtyard, via the gate motif to the rocky scenery and on over the lake folding far in the horizon. It is to the south that the building is looking, to the direction of daytime.

We enter the house from the wrong direction, along the road, which was added only later. Contemporary summer cottage culture is characterised by indolence and laziness. We want easy access by car, the weather must be no hindrance. This is why the lake regions of Finland are filled with public and private roads, and the cars stand uncomfortably near the cottage. The driveway to Muuratsalo is not too near the house, however. By the roadside there are today all sorts of fancy neotraditional one-family houses. I wonder if the residents are aware of the fact that one of the gems of world architecture is located in their neighbourhood? In fact, do they care? Possibly. On the other hand, people should be allowed to realise their own dreams, build the kind of houses they want, construct their own image. This is the philosophy Aalto followed when he built his own summer cottage. We descend along the narrow, meandering path towards the house, devouring the fresh forest air, which purifies our bodies and minds. The forest smells of old rain. Entered from this side, the building has small features, a composition growing gradually out of shacks and outbuildings. The impression is astoundingly different from the one you get when arriving by boat. The massively arching open rock next to the house is of equal importance, or perhaps it has even more. The building seems to seek shelter from it, leaning against it. The primitive man always builds on nature's terms, respecting it and utilising its special features.

By the rock you can sneak into the courtyard, and through it either into the building or to the entrance from the backyard and further inside. The floor plan is a simple L-shape; the bedrooms are located on one side, the living room on the other, while the kitchen and the entrance are in the corner. The bedroom windows are smaller, opening to the backyard towards the pine forest. Should someone come to the house early in the morning, the family can see the visitor from their bedroom. I think it faces east. The master bedroom is situated at the end of the bedroom wing. Unlike the other chambers, it also offers the view to the south described above. Aalto must have loved that view. Beside the bed there is a collection of books on a small shelf, something to read during the holidays. An early volume of Göran Schildt, Vonnegut's novels, and a couple of detective stories.

The living room rises graciously towards the descending slope and the lake, to which there is a little view. At the lower end there is a fireplace and at the higher, a desk, on which there is an old drawing of a boat. Over the desk, in the highest spot, there is a loft. You can reach it by climbing a step ladder. Today, there is little else there than an easel with an unfinished oil painting. The middle of the canvas is painted heavily, lumpily, with white shaded with natural hues and a touch of brown. Either the subject is fully abstract, or it might also represent a natural formation with a minimalistic approach. The clotted surface of the painting invites you to touch. From the loft there is a long, diagonal view over the living room to the fireplace and the entrance door. The living room is reminiscent of a miniature stage.

In a central place in front of the window there is an easy chair. Sitting in it, you can see the long view just described. We enter the door and walk back to the courtyard. Twilight has stolen in, the sun is near the horizon now, right at the vanishing point of the meandering lake. A few minutes more and it has disappeared altogether. In the middle of the courtyard there is a fireplace. For some reason we all gather around it, like primitive men around the campfire. We imagine a blazing fire, lighting its own space in the cold autumn night.

We walk to the sauna along a small path. In the twilight it is hard to see holes or stones. On a path like this it is better to watch your step, letting the sole of your shoe lightly touch the ground all the time. Mie, our Japanese friend, manages well. I ask her if she likes trekking, as she walks with such certainty to the sauna, without stumbling at all. Mie tells me she likes to trek in the mountains back in Japan. We see the sauna now; it is made of round logs, and there is something odd about its shape. In a strange way, it seems to narrow down towards the back. Taking a closer look, we see how the sauna is built, the reason for the wedge-like shape. All wall logs have been set in the same direction, so that they narrow down towards the forest. This creates a charming emphasised perspective, further accentuated by the inclined roof, also due to the narrowing logs. The front wall and the porch are on the wide side, facing the lake. It is pitch dark now and the significance of the porch is hard to discern as we cannot see the lake. I am trying to explain to Mie the monumental significance of the sauna and the sauna porch in Finnish culture. The fact that we cannot see anything makes this somewhat difficult. Yet we can hear the presence of the lake: the tempered waves lapping on the pebbles by the shore.

Säynätsalo

Surrounded by a small green area, the building stands like a fortress. The relatively closed redbrick facade emphasises this impression. Outwardly, the building appears large. The fathers of the parish have something to be proud of. The greenness of nature, now giving way to the grey and brown shades of autumn, strikes a strong complementary to the red brick. The surrounding nature is light, while the building is heavy. The compositional highlight, the high-ceilinged assembly room, conveys power and might. The building seems to give a rumble first, then start a gentle speech on arrival in the inner courtyard. There we ascend along steps, ceremonially, by the side of the assembly room. The other steps, familiar to us from photographs, are nowhere to be seen. Instead, we see a churned heap of earth; the guide tells us that renovations are under way. Cosy and low, the inner courtyard completely differs from the impression given by the exterior. The surrounding corridors open onto the courtyard through large glass windows. The details look somehow weird, exotic. According to an interpretation I once heard, the town hall resembles an Italian farmhouse. This atmosphere is clear. To me, the inner courtyard appears Japanese in some way. I remark on this to Mie, who stops to think about it, puzzled.

Accompanied by a group of foreign guests, Aalto arrives at Säynätsalo in order to present the architecture of the town hall, his justified pride and glory. He sees a neon light, which was definitely not included in his design, and flares up. In the presence of his foreign guests the eminent architect gives a solo show. Gathering some sizeable stones from the ground, he starts throwing them at the neon board.

The grass courtyard leads us to the entrance hall and the redbrick interior. The atmosphere reminds us of a monastery. The morning light sweeps along the heavy redbrick walls, revealing every deviation, protrusion, and recess. The relief-like character and the touch of the human hand inherent in masonry are well presented. I discern a brick bond with two stretchers and one header in the wall. The red brick and the natural light are accompanied by warm wood; wood is wherever we touch a surface. It is a pleasant material to touch. Peeking into the room which housed the town board, we see a long table, heavy chairs, and an amusing chairman's gavel at the end of the table. The atmosphere is solemn, but somehow deserted. The guide tells us that the building today is little more than a museum exhibit. The same fate applies to many sites of architectural value. Unused, they lose their relationship with real life. Besides mere structure, material, light, and space, a good building must be part of real life. If a building lacks this connection, it is not architecture. Yet the Säynätsalo town hall is. Just like masterpieces of earlier centuries, it is a document, telling a story about its own days and the way life was. Buildings left empty like this are a form of archaeology, serving people in their own way.
Like the external composition, the interior spatial series also culminates in the assembly room. The shape of the space must be close to a cubicle: the room is small, yet high. There is little floor area, but a lot of space. I feel as if I were inside a brick:

the sense of material is strong indeed. Light is filtered from the side wall into the room, from high above. The dialogue of light and heavy red brick is extremely intensive in this room. The podium and the benches are made of wood. There is a sacral element in the atmosphere. It is nice to sit on the bench, lost in thought.
We leave the premises, but turn back to take final look. There is something sad to the beauty of the view. Some places make us restless, some may arouse us sexually, some make us sentimental. I don't think these things need to be analysed or explained. But often we do feel something inside us when seeing a beautiful building. To be called a work of art, a building only needs to provide a single person with an experience like that.
Before leaving, we drop in at the library, filled with fresh natural light from above. The most pleasant room in the building is the children's department, where the familiar Aalto furniture can be found in miniature, half-sized. I sit down in a small chair for a moment, wondering what children usually think, or rather experience, inside buildings. Do they find houses too big or themselves too small? I cannot recall these thoughts anymore. But I do remember that when I was a child houses seemed more personal, more alive. Special features, all kinds, had extra emphasis in the eyes of the child. I think the town hall library might be a pleasant experience for a child. There is space and shape, warm hues, small shelves, miniature furniture, and plenty of light.

A Great House in Töysä
On the road again. The rolling Jyväskylä landscape typical of Central Finland has turned straight and smooth. The number of fields compared to forest and lakes has grown. The horizon looms large. In fact, the landscape is nothing more than a horizontal line, broken occasionally by a building, almost invariably simple and large. For the most part, the buildings are barns, standing in the middle of fields with their strongly pitched roofs. The low morning light emphasises the masses of the buildings, making all shapes extra clear. Viewed from the corner, the lighted side clearly differs from the shaded side. The atmosphere is quiet; it reminds me of a Surrealist painting by Chirico. We have now left Central Finland and arrived in Ostrobothnia. Here all the houses are big. In fact, everything around here is bigger: the fields, the barns, the cars, the people. Somewhere here is the largest store in Finland, run by two brothers who even publish a weekly newspaper in their shop. Alvar Aalto was born in Kuortane, here in Southern Ostrobothnia. This may explain something: his grand manners and the straightforward gestures in his buildings. By the roadside we see a sign saying: "Töysä 1 km".
We curve into the courtyard of Terho Manner House. The

Medieval castle, Hämeenlinna.
ハーメンリンナの古城。

symmetric composition and the tall posts by the main entrance contribute to the massive impression. The courtyard gently slopes towards the lake, to where the axis of the house is directed. This is an early work by Aalto, something he designed for a relative. He was not yet famous, and this is obviously why the gestures are so grand. The building is Classicist, huge, and the composition makes it look even bigger than it actually is. It brings to mind grand Italian mansions and cardinals' houses with their water gardens and columns. And yet this is merely a farmhouse in a small Ostrobothnian municipality.

As a young man Aalto boasted to his fellow students that he was going to travel to Sweden and take a summer job at Gunnar Asplund's office; Asplund was already a famous architect, a leader of Classicism in Scandinavia. Off he sailed to Sweden with much ado. Yet in a few days Aalto was back in Finland, making no fuss about his return. Aalto had indeed visited Asplund, who had flatly turned him down.

On the porch we are greeted by the mistress of the house. She is neither big nor pompous, but is very friendly and nice. She tells us she now lives alone in the big house: her husband is dead and her children have moved out. It is hard work to maintain the house, but she says it is easy to keep fit and active as she is never idle. In one of the rooms we see an exercise bike.

The floor plan is symmetrical. All common rooms are downstairs, while the bedrooms are upstairs. The internal order follows that of the traditional Ostrobothnian farmhouse, which was always two-storey in order to achieve a lofty appearance. Moreover, the traditional Ostrobothnian farmhouse was invariably situated on a visible site so as to show off to the neighbours. But as the landscape is flat, the large buildings fit in well. A large farmland landscape requires a large house. In this early work by Aalto these Ostrobothnian features are manifest, mixed with elements from history. The upstairs balcony offers a magnificent view over the fields and the lakes. The atmosphere is tangible, abounding in countryside tradition.

The Wooden Church

Last night can still be felt in our heads and feet. As a break from our Aalto tour, we decide to treat ourselves to a visit to the old wooden church of Petäjävesi. We want to present the traditional craft of timber building to our Japanese friend, offer her some background for Aalto's timber architecture. The church of Petäjävesi stands proudly in the landscape. Its precise geometry is in beautiful contrast to the surrounding nature. The pitched roof, covered with wooden shingles, dominates the surroundings. I tell Jari and Mie that I think about this church every single day. There cannot be a better building. In all the world, this church is among the three greatest sacral buildings. I haven't seen the other two yet.

The basic scheme of the church is symmetrical and cruciform, with the ends some seven metres across. I presume the size derives from the maximum length of the wall logs. The church was designed and built by a carpenter in the 18th century. The design was probably no more than a sketch on a piece of paper, but you can see from the building that it was made with love and craft. At the end there is a bell tower, built by the carpenter's grandson; it fits well into the church. There is a heavy smell of tar in the air. At the weighty wooden door we are met by the church warden, who has promised to show us around. When we enter, the thick floorboards creak under our feet. The boards in the floors, walls, and ceilings are untreated. The low entrance hall with exciting decorative paintings in the ceiling leads us into the church proper. The chamber is splendid. It feels huge, yet tangible, comprehensible. The impression probably derives from the combination of small floor area and ample space. Inside, the pitched roof is clad to form a vault-shaped segmented surface, imitating the vaults of stone churches. The acoustics is like inside a wooden drum. Jari takes a few photographs of the interior. The church warden tells us about the history of the church and shows us some interesting details. The pulpit is like a sculpture, carried by a wooden human figure on its head. The impression is beautiful and amusing. The warden shows us the vestry and the small bench next to the pulpit. In the old days, there was an usher sitting on the bench during the service, sternly watching over the congregation. Should someone fall asleep, which sometimes happened as people travelled to the service from far away early in the morning, the usher would ring a bell next to him. If this did not help, the usher would grab his long stick and give the sleeper a poke in the side. We sit down on the wooden benches and listen to our guide's funny stories. I contemplate the long continuum of architecture. Nothing is ever completely new; the same things always come up in new ways. Modern construction should not differ from traditional construction in any way. While the modern is merely making something old in a novel way, each old building was once new. In order to find new ways of expression, we need to travel in time. We have to visit the past to find the future.

We leave at dusk. The road is icy and very slippery. The Finnish spruce forest by the roadside looks cosy and safe. Mie asks us to sing a Finnish song. Tentatively, we pick out a song made to a poem by Aleksis Kivi, the Finnish national writer and playwright.

Snug the squirrel lies
In his mossy lair
Where no tooth of Frost
Nor the hunter's snare
Have ever reached.

A Vision of a Better World
Anna, the guide, is waiting for us at the entrance to Villa Mairea. This is my second visit here. The building is like a novel or a short story, leading the reader from one incident to other, constantly revealing new surprises and turns; as you progress, the plot is weaved into a complex, intricate narrative. The introduction to Villa Mairea is the surrounding pine forest. Together with the large building, the forest strikes a solemn atmosphere. Yet the wooden entrance canopy and the pavement made of natural stone break the impression of excessive grandiosity; instead, the visitor is brought to the humble atmosphere of a Finnish crofter's cottage. We enter the house. The free-form wall of the entrance hall leads us towards the living room. Should anyone need to use the toilet, it is easy to find following the shape of the wall. The living room offers a view to the courtyard: a forest landscape with a sauna and a pond with a quay. The courtyard is a miniature landscape of a larger model. A complex scenery like this, surrounded by interiors, is reminiscent of old Japanese gardens, which are miniatures of larger landscapes.

In the corner of the living room there is a fireplace of sculptural dimensions. We sit down in the adjacent group of sofa and armchairs. Sitting on the sofa, you can see the forest landscape and the fire at the same time. There is something familiar, primitive about this. The shape of the fireplace is beautiful. It is enlivened with organic details carved in the white stone; they are like handprints on a pillow. The staircase is a peculiar bamboo construction. It gives an impression of a sort of hut in the woods. There is something exotic to the staircase, it is familiar and foreign at the same time. The steps are well-carved, especially the one closest to the floor: I cannot resist the temptation to go and touch it. The rounded wood feels nice under the foot. Already as a child I was interested in the personal, touchable details of buildings. But the grown-up world tends to discard spontaneity, as if steps were meant for treading only; but as children we discovered several functions for stairs when we were playing. I climb upstairs to the bedrooms. Sleeping in these bedrooms must feel like sleeping under the stars. I wonder if this impression derives from the large windows, from the impression of space, or from the small post placed in the middle of the rooms. Perhaps from all of these. The highlight of the 2nd floor is the studio of the mistress of the house, opening towards the courtyard through large windows. This is a good place for observing what is going on in the house and its surroundings: it is the highest spot in the house. This must now be the wooden emphasis in the mass, familiar from so many photographs. The small wooden maritime ladders lead to the gallery of the high-ceilinged studio. There I find a pile of old straw hats.

We go back downstairs. The kitchen is spacious and cosy, attracting people to stay and chat more than the dining room. The view to the forest is pleasant. Through the dining room there is an exit out to under an interesting canopy, where there is a fireplace laid of slates. The side of the fireplace has steps leading up to a roof terrace. In compliance with tradition, access to the sauna is from the outside. With its canopy and terrace opening towards the pool, the sauna resembles a simple summer cottage sauna. The free-form swimming pool resembles a small forest pond. During my last visit here I took a swim and noticed that even the bottom is free-form.

It is twilight. We leave the courtyard and exit through the house. I notice beautiful paintings on the walls. The house conveys a strong feeling of its occupants, Harry and Maire Gullichsen: of their values, their lifestyle, their philosophy. An alliance like this, of an unbiased, liberal client and a good architect, is exceptional indeed. The result is a *Gesamtkunstwerk*, a joint creation by the client and the architect. Villa Mairea renders a faith in the happy union of man and nature, tradition and the modern way of life. Yet despite all the loftiness, the building bears a strong resemblance to a common Finnish home; it has warmth. For Aalto and the Gullichsens, all of them reformists, Villa Mairea signified a vision of a better world.

Aalto and the mistress of Villa Mairea were close, sometimes even too close. Sigfried Giedion, the historian once visited the house. He found it to be against all he advocated in his writings. He said to Aalto: "You haven't made a building. You've made a love poem."

Airborne Again
We have finished our tour. We have said goodbye at the airport. Jari has returned home to Kumpula. Mie has taken a plane to Tokyo; the bow carried an image of Moomintroll. I am sitting in a plane to London; this bow has Santa Claus painted on it. The week was an intensive one, and I feel a sort of post-journey melancholy creeping in. I look out through the small window. The lakes and rivers meander like Aalto's houses.

(Translated from Finnish by Laura Mänki)

Note: Extract from Aleksis Kivi's poem translated by Keith Bosley, published in *Odes* (Finnish Literature Society, Helsinki 1994)

「私は建てる」こんな覚えやすい言葉が建築家アルヴァ・アアルトのモットーであった。彼はまれに見る働き者であり、その長い生涯に300件以上にものぼる建物を実現した。その中には、小さなサマー・コテージもあれば壮大な公共建築もあるといった具合に、彼が手掛けたものはドアの取手から都市計画にまで及んだ。

今日ではアルヴァ・アアルトに関する話、研究、書籍や出版物もまた無数にある。彼の功績を称え、メダルや記念硬貨、シンポジウムにもその名は冠されている。フィンランドの50マルッカ紙幣には、片面にフィンランディア・ホールの絵柄、その裏面にはちょっと空を見上げるこの建築家の肖像画が刷り込まれている。どの建築家についても客観的な目で見なければならないが、ことアアルトに対してはなかなかそうもいかない。同じくらい困難なのは、主観的な態度をとることである。しかもそうする以外に、与えられた建物の領域へ入る方法はない。アアルトの場合は、残念ながらその領域がどのようなものかがたいがい予測されてしまうようだ。その領域には厳しく教条化されたいかにも宗教のようなところがあり、答を与えるだけで疑問を抱いたり発見する余地をまったく残してくれない。

ぼくたち若い建築家にとって、アアルトは同時代の建築家ではない。ぼくらが抱く彼の人物像とは、個人的な思いもなければ完結されてもいない、ごくごく断片的なものである。生前のこの建築家の作品を分析することはたやすいことではない。氾濫する情報を丹念に調べなければならないというのが、その理由だ。何しろこれまで言葉や文章になったものすべてが対象となるわけだから。建築のエッセンスは、往々にしてメディアの渦に呑み込まれてしまう。何度も何度もあらゆるメディアで紹介されたものを、客観的に扱うことは無理だ。そのうえ、アアルトのイメージはもっぱら彼の人間性に基づいている。それもうなずける。なぜなら、アアルトはカリスマ性をもった人物であったと思われるからだ。彼自身、世間一般の傾向として、人間性とその人の功績とを混同してしまうことを百も承知していたにちがいない。晩年になって、彼は伝記作家にこう忠告したことがあった。「建築について書くんだよ。私のことではなくね」

「私は建てる」という言葉には、この建築家の作品のまぎれもない本質が隠されている。実存する建物が、アアルトの功績をありのままに伝えてくれる。時代は変わり、若い世代は旅をする機会を得た。今では船も列車も飛行機もある。自分自身で建築を理解するには、文字を通してではなく、自分の目と耳と鼻と手を使うことが最も有効である。というのも、建物は人間の生活の一部となってこそ、初めて意義をもつからだ。本稿ではそんな旅について書いてみた。アルヴァ・アアルトの住宅を訪ねてまわったときの、ある個人的な旅である。

機上から

空から眺めたフィンランドは、十分わかりやすい風景に映る。緑色の絨毯のような森林は、美しいうねりを見せる湖や川の青色の部分で切断される。陸の等高線に沿って走る道路は、まるで紙テープがほどけて転がっているようだ。けれど何よりも優雅な輪郭を描くのは湖岸線だ。その輪郭は、長い年月を経て湖水に浸食され、連続的で柔らかい線になっている。建物の小さな集合体となって見えるのが村だ。そのほとんどは道路や川沿い、あるいは湖畔にある。ときどき村の中央にそびえ立つ建物を見つけては、それが教会だと確認できる。町や都市は、森林や湖沼の面積に比べると驚くほど少ない。機上から眺めるかぎり、現実には諸々の問題や失敗があるにもかかわらず、それらを風景から読み取ることはできない。フィンランドもヨーロッパ大陸とまったく同じような環境問題を抱えており、また自然保護はしばしば危機にさらされている。ところが飛行機の窓から覗くと、その風景には独創性とうるわしさがある。ぼくはコーヒーとカルヴァドスを注文し、先週の出来事を振り返っているところだ。

ヘルシンキでの食事

ぼくたちの旅はアルヴァ・アアルトの設計したレストラン、サヴォイでスタートした。ぼくの事務所では、ちょうど大掛かりなコンペの応募案を完成させ、締め切りに間に合わせて郵送したところだ。コンペはフィンランドの建築家にとっては根強い伝統として受け継がれてきたものであり、そしてコンペ後の打ち上げパーティもそうだ。日本からの友人、ミエはちょうど東京から到着したばかりで、ぼくらと合流した。ぼくたちがレストランに入ったときには、ほとんど客の姿もなく、隅のテーブルで、一組のビジネスマンがコーヒーやコニャックを片手に雑談をしているくらいだった。この空間で強烈に印象的なのは、なんといっても冬めいた街を照らす光だ。その光が、ヘルシンキのまた違った側面を浮かび上がらせる。ガラス貼りの面が多いので、どの方向にも見通しがきく。サヴォイ・レストランは、街を水平に眺め渡すことのできる数少ない貴重な場所である。内装は木を基調としており、品がある。木製の仕上げと景観との関係こそが、レストランの居心地の良さばかりでなく、格調高さと大陸的な雰囲気も与えている。ロビーも気持ちの良い空間だ。このレストランは、建築家と施主との協力が良い結果を得た好例だと思う。要するに名建築には名建築家だけでなく、施主と施工者もそうでなくてはならないのである。サヴォイ・レストランを注文したアハルストリョム社は模範的な施主であった。天井と壁に張られた合板は、フィンランドの林業を暗示するが、アハルストリョム社は当時も今もこの業界の一員である。

メニューは昔とほとんど変わらないままのようだ。ぼくらは食前酒としてキイチゴのリキュール入りウォッカを、それからビール数本と氷水も注文した。ウェイターはこのレストランの伝統も評判も十分心得ているらしい。最初のコースに、ぼくたちは生鮭と白身魚の酢漬けを食べた。それは、釣りに夢中で刺身には目がないと言う日本の友人への友好のしるしである。

会話がはずむにつれ、その場のテンションがだんだんと高まり、この空間さえも小さく感じられるようになった。低く吊るされたランプの光がまっすぐテーブルにあたる。形の良いドーム状のかさからこぼれる光が、テーブルのあたりを演出してくれる。周りのテーブルもレストランも姿を消し、まるで目の前のテーブルと自分の仲間だけになったように思える。照明のおかげで、たとえ8人いようと、ぼくたちの一人一人が進んで話の輪に入ることができる。メイン・コースにはマンネルハイム元帥を偲んでフォールシュマック（訳註：ヨーロッパ北部に伝統的な料理。羊挽肉をベースに、アンチョビやマッシュポテト、キュウリ、ビーツ等を加え

たオーブン料理)を注文した。言い伝えによれば、彼はここの常連であった。食事を終えてからも、ぼくらは数時間ばかりブランデーをすすりながら長居をし、客のいないレストランで心おきなく静かな時間を過ごした。仲間の一人がアアルトの逸話を語ってくれた。

> オタニエミのキャンパスは、のちにアアルトが実現することになったけれども、その企画会議が開かれたのが、このサヴォイというわけだ。アアルトは主席建築家の候補に挙がっていた。ところが会議はひどい騒ぎに発展していって、とうとう本格的な喧嘩になってしまった。アアルトの助手の一人が施主の踝に嚙み付いて叫んだそうだ。「建築のためを思うなら、この仕事はアアルトに任せろ!」って。

ぼくたちは支払いを済ませた。昨今のレストランでは、統一された内装というものはあまり見かけない光景だ。そんなことが課題になるのは、たいていロック・スターや外資系のチェーン店くらいのものだ。ともかくぼくらは、いま初めて建築家アアルトと遭遇したわけだ。

赤煉瓦への序

フィンランドの凍てついた農地は美しい。秋の朝は陽射しが弱いけれど、淡い色彩をみせる自然界の微妙なニュアンスを見るには十分な明るさだ。わずかな光の中、風景のシルエットは彫塑的で神々しい姿にまとまっている。それを車窓越しに追うのが楽しい。この秋を迎えてから初めて凍えるような夜が続いたので、野原は霜のヴェールで覆われている。今回の旅のメンバーは、ぼくたち3人だ。ヤリは助手席にミエが乗っているので慎重に運転している。いっぽうぼくは後部座席から状況を追っている。道路は滑りやすくなっているのに、この車についているのは夏用タイヤだ。けれど、ぼくらはゆったりしたペースで進む。ぼくらにはいくらでも時間はあるのだから。

最初の目的地はユヴァスキュラだ。その前にハーメンリンナに立ち寄り、中世の城でコーヒーを飲んだ。平日なので、観光客はバス・ツアーでやってきた年金受給者ばかりだ。ぼくらはガイドつきのツアーにまぎれ込んで、中世の展示物を見学した。そして城の煉瓦積みを見て感服した。煉瓦積みの壁は、当時の建築としては第一級だ。当時の人々は、些細なディテールにこだわることなどなかった。この地方の人たちは、おっとりした気質で知られるが、彼らはそうした土地に育まれた風習を踏襲しながら常識的でみごとな建物をつくりあげた。地面から立ち上がる壁は巨大な石で始まり、やがて小ぶりな石に続き、最上部では小さな煉瓦になっている。こうした石を持ち上げるには多大な労力を要したにちがいない。だから高い位置ほど軽い材料が使われたのだろう。城壁は傾斜し、なだらかに膨らんでいる。床はどこもわずかに勾配がついている。人間の手でつくり上げられたものが、長い歴史を経て今も遍在する。

ヤリがぼくらを小さな礼拝堂へ案内してくれた。およそ10m×10mほどの広さの室内は石造で、そこには複数の窓や、ベンチ、そして祭壇がある。自然光に溢れているし、全体としては美しい印象を受けたが、といって華美ではない。ハーメンリンナは煉瓦建築のための良い前置きとなった。今日の我々のテーマは煉瓦だということになり、ぼくたちはユヴァスキュラへ、そしてアアルトが手掛けた煉瓦づくりの建物に向けて旅を続ける。

サマー・コテージにて

赤煉瓦の建物が、古色を帯びた白い外観を呈し、フィンランドらしい湖畔の景観の中に昂然と屹立している。そのいっぽうでこの建物は景観に溶け込んでいるため、遠景ではその一部分しか見ることができない。ムーラッツァロにある住宅、すなわちこの建築家のサマー・コテージは、ころころと表情を変える。一見すると壮大であり、華やかですらある。そこでは高く突き出た居間兼アトリエと中庭の隅にあるゲートを中心として全体が結晶化している。つづいて現れるのが、その反対にちょっとした特徴やディテールだが、かえって全体のバランスがとれ、面白味が出ている。こうした構成は脚本と似ている。つまり最初に何か衝撃的な科白があって、その後静めたり和らげる何らかの作用によって一件落着するつくりだ。この特色があるからこそ、ムーラッツァロの別荘は人間味に溢れながらも鮮烈な印象を与えるのだ。

今ここで論じているのは、サマー・コテージであることを忘れないでほしい。サマー・コテージは、フィンランド人の財産とでも言える伝統なのだから。無性に自然と一つになりたくなったとき、フィンランド人は自分のサマー・コテージに行けばその欲望を満たすことができる。独特なやり方ではあるが、ムーラッツァロの別荘はこうした自然に対する熱情を受け止めてくれる。湖から、ボートを漕いでこの建物に近づいていく。まずはイントロだ。湖水、なだらかにうねる森、そしてぴしゃぴしゃと丸い小石を洗う波。岸へ着くと、木の根っこや石に足をとられながら別荘に向かって登って行く。まるで儀式のようだ。中庭は、この建物のいわばゲートである。設計者は、コテージの導入部を古代風にすることを想定していた。いろいろな積まれ方をした煉瓦や実験的なタイルの貼り方は、この別荘のあるじについて物語っている。つまり、彼は七つの海を航海し、経験を積んだ人であると。それでいて、どこにでもあるようなサマー・コテージもが思い出される。フィンランド人ならばほとんど誰でも、楽しみながら自らの手でサマー・コテージを建てるし、それはこの国では珍しいことでもない。中庭の一角が高くなっているが、これには何ら機能はない。実際のところ、このせいで湖への眺めは塞がれている。それについては、こんな話がある。

> 石工とアアルトは作業を始めた。「さあとりかかって。私が指示するまで手を休めないように」アアルトは石工に告げると切り株に腰を下ろし、コシュケンコルヴァ・ウォッカの栓を抜いた。2本目を空にした彼は、うたた寝を始めた。目を覚ますと、石工の仕事はすっかりはかどっていて、ちょうど今ある高さにまで達していた。アアルトはとび起き、叫んだ。「おい君、すごい才能だな!」

湖寄りの壁には開口部があり、そこからムーラメの教会の鐘楼を指差すことができる。どのみち別荘は、湖の景色を見渡すようには西側を向いていないのかもしれない。けれども代わりに、狭く曲がりくねった入江を見下ろすようにして南の方角に向いている。その大昔につくられた入江の線は、建築家の思いがたっぷり込められたサヴォイ花瓶になんと似ていることだろう。この別荘は連

Wooden Church, Petäjävesi.
ペタヤヴェシの木造教会。

続した空間からなるが、居間が位置するのはその最後尾（先頭ともいえるが）である。居間からは、大きなガラス窓越しに中庭を眺めることができる。そしてゲートのモティーフ越しには、岩の多い景色が見え、さらに遥か彼方の水平線では湖が断ち切れているのがわかる。ともかく建物の正面は南側である。したがって建物は昼の方角を向くわけだ。

ぼくたちは、本来とは違う方向の道路側から別荘に入る。この入口は後から付け加えられたにすぎない。現代のサマー・コテージ文化を言い表わすなら、怠惰とか不精といった言葉になる。別荘の目の前まで車で行きたい、天候に左右されたくない、と思うのがぼくら現代人だ。だからフィンランドの湖沼地帯は公道や私道で埋め尽くされているし、車は見苦しくも別荘のすぐそばに停めてある。だがムーラッツァロの別荘では、車寄せと建物とは接近しすぎることはない。今日この沿道には家族向け住宅が建ち並ぶが、それらは様々な趣向が凝らされた新伝統主義的なものだ。はたしてそこの住人たちは、珠玉の名建築が近くにあることを知っているのだろうか。実際、この人たちは気にかけるだろうか。あるいはそうかもしれない。翻って考えると、この人たちにもそれぞれの夢を実現させる権利はあるのだから、好きなように家を建てる自由はあるわけだ。この原理に則ってアアルトは自分のサマー・コテージを建てた。ぼくたちは、曲がりくねった細い小道を歩きながら、新鮮な林の空気を胸一杯に吸い込んで身も心も清め、そして別荘へと下りて行った。林はだいぶ前に降った雨のせいで、じめついた匂いがする。この方角から別荘の敷地に入ると、この建物らしいちょっとした特徴が顔を覗かせ、丸太小屋や薪小屋があるあたりからしだいに全体の構成が読めてくる。これが同じ建物かと目を疑うほど、ボートで来たときの印象とは異なる。アーチ形に穴の開いた岩が、どっしりと別荘の脇に横たわっている。この岩も建物に匹敵するくらい重要なものだ。むしろ岩の方が重要かもしれない。建物は岩陰に隠れるかのようにして、そちらに寄り添っている。原始人は必ず自然の摂理に従って建物を建てていたし、自然を尊重することも、その特性を利用することも忘れなかった。

岩の脇を抜けると中庭へ忍び込むことができる。中庭を抜ければ、建物の内部、もしくは裏庭に面した玄関から建物の奥に入ることができる。平面は単純なL字型をしており、その一翼には寝室群、もう一翼には居間、そして角にはキッチンと玄関がおかれている。寝室に穿たれた小さめの窓からは、裏庭とその奥の松林が見える。万が一朝早くに誰かが訪れても、ここに住む家族は寝室から誰が来たのかを確認できる。窓はどうやら東に向いているようだ。主寝室は寝室翼の先端にある。ほかの部屋には前述した南側への眺望がないが、この部屋にはある。アアルトはさぞかしこの眺めが気に入ったのだろう。ベッド脇の小さな本棚には、休暇中の読書に備えて本が揃えられている。ヨーラン・シルツの初期の著作やヴォネガットの小説、それに推理小説が二、三冊ある。

居間の天井はたおやかに傾斜している。この天井は湖や下り坂道に向かって上昇するので、これらの景色はあまり見えない。天井の低い側には暖炉があり、その反対側には机がおかれている。机の上には昔描かれたボートの図面がある。机の真上を見上げると、部屋の最上部にロフトがある。段梯子を上ればロフトだ。現在のロフトには、イーゼルとその上に架けられた描きかけの油彩画しかない。キャンヴァスの中央は、白っぽい自然色で厚ぼったく塗られ、そこに茶色で一筆加えられている。この絵画の主題は、まったくの抽象であるか、もしくは自然の形態をミニマル芸術風に表現したものであろう。凝固した絵の具を見ると、思わずキャンヴァスをなでてみたくなる。ロフトから対角線方向に居間を見下ろすと、奥の暖炉やその向こうの玄関扉まで見通すことができる。この居間からは、小型の舞台装置が連想される。

窓辺の中央には安楽椅子がある。そこに腰掛けると、今説明したとおりに奥まで見通すことができる。ぼくらは扉を開けて中庭に戻った。いつしか黄昏時になり、日が水平線にさしかかっている。そこはちょうど蛇行する湖が途切れる位置だ。数分後には何も見えなくなった。中庭の中央には炉がある。どうしたわけか、まるで篝火を囲む原始人のようにぼくらはその周りを取り囲んだ。そして秋の夜寒に震えながら、ぼくらは思った。赤々と燃える火が、その場を明るくしてくれているのだと。

ぼくたちは小道を辿ってサウナ小屋に向かった。薄暗がりの中だと、地面のへこみや転がっている石には気づきにくい。こんな道を歩くときは、足元に気をつけながら、常に靴の底で地面をなでるようにして歩いたほうがいい。日本から来た仲間、ミエはなんなくやってのける。そんなふうに彼女がサウナ小屋目指し、つまずきもせずに確実な足取りで歩いていくので、彼女にトレッキングは好きかい？と尋ねた。日本ではよく山歩きに出掛けるけれど、とミエは答えた。サウナ小屋が見えてきた。丸太積みの小屋は、どこかいびつな形をしている。この小屋は見慣れないつくりをしており、奥に行くにしたがってすぼまっているようだ。ぼくらはさらに近寄って、サウナ小屋がどのように建てられ、なぜ楔形をしているのかを調べてみた。つまり丸太材をすべて同じ向きに積んで壁をつくっているので、建物が林側ですぼんでいるわけだ。こうするとパースが強くかかるし、それに愛嬌もある。しかも屋根が傾いて載っていたり、先細の丸太材が使われることで、そのパースがいっそう目立つ。小屋の幅広になっている側には、湖に面して正面の壁とポーチがある。あたりが急に暗くなり、湖が見えないので、ポーチの趣旨が読み取りにくい。フィンランドの文化にとってなぜサウナやサウナ・ポーチが歴史的な重みがあるのかを、ミエに説明しようと思った。けれども、何も見えない状況ではいささか困難だ。それでも湖の気配は感じられる。耳をすませば、穏やかな波が打ち際の小石を洗うのがわかる。

セイナッツァロ

狭い緑地の中に、さながら要塞のごとく建物が建っている。わりに閉鎖的な赤煉瓦のファサードが、さらにその印象を強めている。見たところは大きな建物だ。この教区の神父にとっても、ちょっとした自慢の種だ。自然の緑が、今は秋らしいくすんだ茶褐色になっているが、煉瓦の赤に対してはっきりとした補色を見せている。周りの自然は軽やかなのに、建物は重々しい。全体の構成の中でひときわ目を引くのが、天井高のある議場だ。そこには権威と力が示されている。建物はまず最初にごうごうと唸り声をあげ、それから穏やかな話し方で中庭に迎え入れるようにも思える。ぼくたちは中庭を抜け、議場の脇にあ

る階段を粛々と上った。ぼくらがよく写真で見かける階段は、これとは別だが、そちらはどこにも見当たらない。その代わりに僕たちが目にしたのは、荒々しく掘り起こされた土の山だ。ガイドの説明によれば、現在は修復工事中らしい。中庭はこぢんまりとしていて落ち着いているので、外観とはまったく異なる印象を与える。中庭を囲む廊下は、大きなガラス窓で中庭側に開かれている。なぜかディテールが奇妙で異国風なデザインに思える。かつて耳にした一説によれば、この村役場にはイタリアの農家の面影があるらしい。ここでは空気が澄みきって感じられる。中庭にはいくらか日本的なところがあるように思えたので、それをミエに話すと、彼女は当惑してしばらく考え込んでしまった。

　外国からの来客に村役場の建築を見せようと、アアルトは彼らを引き連れセイナッツァロに到着した。この建物は、彼の誇りと栄誉の証しだ。アアルトはネオン灯を目にすると、かっとなった。彼の設計にネオン灯が含まれたことなど断じてなかった。外国からの来客を前にして、この巨匠は一人舞台を演じた。彼はかなり大きな石を拾い集めると、つぎつぎとネオンサインに投げつけたのだ。

ぼくたちは草の茂る中庭から入口ホールへ、そして赤煉瓦でできた内部空間へと進んだ。内部は僧院の佇まいを思わせる。ずっしりとした壁の表面に朝日がさっと射すと、煉瓦の歪みや凹凸がひとつひとつくっきりと浮かび上がった。そこには、煉瓦積みならではのレリーフ的な性格や手づくりの味わいがみごとに表われている。壁を見れば煉瓦が長手2個と小口1個の単位で積まれているのがわかる。赤煉瓦と自然光には、暖かみのある木が添えられている。どこを触れても木の仕上げになっている。木は心地よい触感をもつ素材だ。議員室をちらっと覗いてみると、そこには長いテーブルと重々しい椅子がある。それからテーブルの端には、議長用の可笑しな木槌がおかれている。議員室には物々しい空気が流れているのに、なぜかさびれた様子でもあった。ガイドの話では、いまやこの建物は博物館の展示にすぎないらしい。かつては名建築のあった場所が、同じような運命を辿ることも少なくない。そうした建物は使用されなくなると、現実の生活との接点を失ってしまうのだ。良い建物であるためには、単に構造、材料、光、空間の良さばかりでなく、人々の生活の一部であることも必要な条件である。この接点をなくした建物は、建築たりえない。しかしセイナッツァロの村役場は建築である。今世紀以前の名作がそうであるように、この建物は史料として、当時の時代背景や暮らしを伝えている。同じように空屋になった建物も、考古学の一形態として、それぞれの特性を活かした貢献をしている。

外観の構成と同じように、連続した内部空間も議場において最高潮に達する。この空間の形状は、ほぼ大部屋の中を仕切ってできた小寝室に近いはずだ。部屋自体は狭く、それでいて高さはある。床面積は小さいが、空間は広い。まるで煉瓦に閉じ込められた気分になるくらいに、材料そのものの存在感が強い。光は側壁のずっと上方から室内に洩れている。ずっしりとした赤煉瓦と光との対話が、この部屋ではますます賑やかになる。演壇と座席は木でできている。ここには聖礼空間のような香りがある。ベンチに掛けて瞑想に耽るのも悪くない。

ぼくたちは構内を出てからも、最後にもう一目見ようと振り返った。この美しい光景には、どこか物哀しさがある。不安を抱かせるところもあれば、性的な刺激もあり、また感傷的なところもある。かといってこうした事柄を分析したり説明する必要もないと思う。それよりも、素晴らしい建物を見れば、たいがい胸の奥底には何かを感じるものだ。一人の人間にこうした体験を与えるだけで、その建物は芸術品の名に値する。

出発前に、ぼくたちは図書館に立ち寄った。そこは、上方からの爽やかな陽射しに満ちている。この建物でいちばん心地よい場所が、この児童書コーナーだ。お馴染みのアアルトの家具は、二分の一の大きさになって置かれている。ぼくはしばらくこの小さな椅子に腰掛け、想像してみた。子供たちはいつもどんなふうに感じるのか、いやむしろこの建物でどんな体験をするのだろうか。子供たちにとって、自分たちの家は大きすぎるだろうか、それとも小さすぎるだろうかと。今となっては思い出せない。ただそれでも憶えているのは、子供だったぼくにとって、家はもっと個人的なもので、生き生きとして見えたことだ。ありとあらゆる特徴は、子供の目には甚だ目立って見えたものだ。この図書館ならば、子供は楽しく過ごせるかもしれない。ここには、空間と形態、暖かみのある色彩、小ぶりの書棚、小型の家具、それにさんさんと降り注ぐ光があるのだから。

トゥーザの邸宅

ふたたび車で移動だ。ユヴァスキュラではフィンランド中部に典型的な起伏のある風景が続いていたが、それがまっすぐで平坦な風景に変わった。森と湖に比べ、田畑の割合が増えてきた。地平線がおぼろげに見える。景色といっても、要するにただただ地平線が続くだけだ。たまに地平線を遮るように立つ建物が見えるが、どれもおしなべて素気なくて大きい。建物の大部分は急勾配屋根の納屋で、畑の真中に佇んでいる。まだ低い朝の陽射しで、建物の量感が強調され、輪郭の一つ一つがひときわくっきりと見える。建物の角の方向から眺めると、光のあたる面と影になった面とではまったく異なる。静けさが漂う。ぼくは、キリコによるシュルレアリスムの絵画を思い出した。ぼくらはフィンランド中部を抜け、オストロボスニア地方に到着したところだ。この地方の住宅はどれも大きい。もっと言うなら、このあたりの畑も納屋も車も人も、なにもかもが大きく見える。この地方のどこかに、フィンランド随一の大きな店があるらしい。その店の経営者である兄弟は、週刊新聞さえも発行し、自分たちの店に置いているという。アルヴァ・アアルトが生まれたのは、このオストロボスニア地方南部のクオルタネだ。彼の作品にみられる大胆さや率直な態度は、ここに由来するのかもしれない。道端の標識には「トゥーザまで1km」とある。ぼくたちはカーヴを曲がり、テルホ・マンネル邸の中庭に到着した。シンメトリーの構成と正面入口脇の背の高い柱のせいで、重厚な印象を受ける。中庭は湖に向かって傾斜している。家の軸線はまっすぐこの湖を指している。これはアアルトの初期の作品で、彼の親類のために設計された。そのころのアアルトがまだ無名だったことを考えれば、これほど立派な外観がつくられたのも納得がいく。この古典主義的で巨大な建物が、実際よりも大きく見えるのは、その

Finnish landscape.
フィンランドの風景。

構成の仕方にある。そこで思い浮かぶのは、豪奢なイタリアの邸宅や枢機卿の屋敷である。なかでもそうした邸宅にみられるウォーター・ガーデンであるとか列柱に通ずる。とはいえ、この家はオストロボスニア地方のただの農家にすぎない。

青年アアルトは、同級生らにこう自慢した。自分はスウェーデンに行き、夏休みはグンナー・アスプルンドの事務所で働く予定だと。当時のアスプルンドは、北欧における古典主義の旗手としてすでに名を成していた。アアルトは大騒ぎの末、やっとの思いでスウェーデン行きの船に乗り込んだ。ところが数日後に彼はフィンランドに戻っており、この帰国について不平も鳴らさなかった。アアルトは現にアスプルンドを訪ねはしたのだが、にべもなく断られたのである。

この家の女主人が玄関でぼくらを迎えてくれた。彼女は大柄でもなければ派手さもないけれど、とても愛想の良い親切な女性である。彼女は夫を亡くし、子供たちも独立したので、今はこの大きな家に独り住まいだと話してくれた。家の維持は大変な仕事だが、彼女いわく、きちんと物の手入れをしていつでも使えるようにしておくことは、さして苦にならないそうだ。それほど彼女は少しも無駄な時間を過ごすことがない人なのだ。ある部屋でぼくたちはサイクリング・マシンを見かけた。

間取りは左右対称である。共有室はすべて下の階、寝室群は上の階にある。内部空間の配置は、伝統的なオストロボスニア地方の農家を下敷きにしている。こうした農家は、背を高く見せるために必ず2階建になっている。しかも近所に見せつけるばかりに、きまって人目にふれる場所に建っている。もっとも、平坦な地形なので大きな建物はうまく馴染んでいる。農地が広がる風景には、大きな家があったほうがいい。このアアルトの初期作には、歴史から引用した要素と織り混ぜられて、こうしたオストロボスニア的な特徴が顕在している。2階のバルコニーからは、眼下に田畑と湖の壮大な眺めが広がる。ここには地方の伝統が色濃く出ており、触れてわかるような雰囲気がある。

木造教会

昨夜の感触が、まだぼくたちの頭にも足にも残っている。ぼくらはアアルト巡りの途中で小休止して、ペタヤヴェシの古い木造教会を見学することにした。丸太組の建物の伝統技能を見てもらえば、日本の友人にもアアルトの木造建築の背景が何かしらわかってもらえるだろう。ペタヤヴェシの教会は、風景の中に威容を誇るようにして建っている。建物に施された精密な幾何学が、周りの自然と見事な対比をなしている。こけら葺きの勾配屋根がひときわ高くそびえる。ヤリとミエに、ぼくがこの教会のことを思わない日はない、と話した。これを上回る建物があるはずはない。世界の三大宗教建築を挙げるとすれば、この教会は3本の指に入る。あとの二つにはまだ巡り合っていない。

教会の平面は、左右対称の十字形をしており、腕の部分は幅がおよそ7mである。ぼくの推測では、この寸法は壁に使われる丸太材の最大長さからきている。18世紀にこの教会を設計し建設したのは、当時の棟梁である。設計と言っても、おそらく一枚の紙きれに描かれたスケッチ程度にすぎないが、この建物を見れ

ば、それが愛情と職人の技から生まれたことがわかる。建物端部にある鐘楼はこの棟梁の孫によるものだが、教会ときれいに調和している。タールのきつい匂いが漂う。重厚な木製扉の前には、この教会の管理人が待っている。ぼくたちの案内役を引き受けてくれた人だ。内部に入ると、足元で床板のきしむ音がした。床や壁や天井に使われている板には、何も処理が施されていない。ぼくたちは入口ホールに入ると、その低い天井に描かれた装飾的な絵画に見入った。そこから招き入れられるようにして本堂へと進んだ。みごとな室内である。かなりの広さを感じさせるのに、実際に身体で感じることのできるし、わかりやすい空間だ。おそらく床面積の狭さと空間の広さとの関係からくるのであろう。勾配屋根の内側には、ヴォールト状の弓形に下見が張られており、石造教会のヴォールト天井が模倣されている。教会の内部は、さながら木太鼓の中のように音が響く。

ヤリが内観を撮影する。管理人がこの教会の由来を聞かせてくれたり、いくつか興味深いディテールを見せてくれた。彫刻のような説教壇が、木彫の人物像に載っている。それが絶妙で面白い効果を上げている。それから説教壇の右手にある祭具室と小さなベンチも見せてもらった。昔は礼拝中に案内人がこのベンチに着き、集会を厳しく監視していたという。もしも居眠りをする者がいたなら、その人の耳元で案内人がベルを鳴らしたそうだ。と言っても、礼拝に参列するために人々は遠方から朝早く家を出て来なければならなかったので、時々そんなことはあった。ベルでも効き目がないと案内人は専用の棒を手に、眠っている人の脇腹を突いた。ぼくたちはそれぞれ木製のベンチに座り、管理人の笑い話に耳を傾けた。ぼくはじっと黙って建築の変遷について考えた。まったく新しいものなど存在しない。要するに、同じことが形を変えて繰り返されるだけだ。現代の建物がどうあろうと、伝統的なものと変わらないはずである。現代の建物といっても、単に旧来のものを新しく作り変えただけのことだ。いっぽう、どんな旧い建物にもかつては新しい時があった。新しい表現方法をみつけるには、ぜひ時間旅行に出掛けるべきだ。ぼくたちは未来を求めて、過去を訪れなければならない。

そこを発つ頃には夕暮になっていた。道路は凍り、滑りやすくなっている。道路脇のドイツトウヒの林が、こぢんまりとして安らげそうな場所に思える。ミエがぼくら二人にフィンランドの歌をリクエストした。とりあえずぼくらが選んでみたのは、劇作家にしてフィンランドの文豪アレクシス・キヴィの詩につけられた節だ。

　リスがぬくぬく寝そべるは
　苔むすねぐら
　霜柱もなければ
　猟師の罠さえ
　届きはしない

より良い世界へのヴィジョン

ガイドのアンナが、ヴィラ・マイレアの玄関でぼくらの到着を待っていた。ぼ

くにとっては二度目の訪問だ。建物はさながら小説や短編小説のように、読者を次々と別の事件に引き込み、新たな驚きや展開を立て続けに披露する。読者が読み進むにつれ、小説の筋は複雑で錯綜した物語の中に織り込まれていく。ヴィラ・マイレアの入口付近は、松林に囲われている。林は大きな建物とともに、厳かな雰囲気を漂わせている。それでも大仰になりすぎないのは、玄関の木造のキャノピーやそこに敷かれた天然石で中和されるからだ。それどころか、むしろフィンランドの慎ましい小作人の家を訪れたような気分になる。ぼくらは家の中へ入った。玄関ホールからフリー・フォームの壁面をつたって行くと、そこは居間だ。たとえトイレを探すことがあっても、壁の線をなぞれば楽に見つかる。居間は中庭に面している。目の前には森林の景色があり、そこにはサウナそしてコンクリート壁をまわした池が配されている。中庭は自然風景の縮写である。このように建物の内側に風景的な諸要素を配した点は、箱庭的な日本庭園を連想させる。

居間の隅には彫刻的な暖炉がある。ぼくたちはそれぞれ暖炉の周りに並べられたソファや肘掛け椅子に腰を下ろした。ソファに座ったまま、森林の風景と暖炉の炎を同時に楽しむことができる。その光景には、どこかで見かけたような原始的な感じがある。暖炉のデザインが素晴らしい。暖炉の白い石材は表面がえぐられ、人を楽しませるような有機的なディテールが施されている。まるで枕についた手の跡のようだ。階段は独特な竹材を使ったつくりだ。これが森の小屋とでもいった風情を出している。階段には妙に風変わりなところがあり、それは見慣れたようでありながらも異国的である。踏段はきれいな形に彫られており、なかでも一番下の段がそうだ。階段に近寄り、つい手を触れずにはいられない。丸みを帯びた木の触感が足に心地よい。まだ子供だったぼくは、建物の中で直接自分で触れることのできるディテールに惹かれた。けれども大人の世界では、踏面に足を載せる以外はしないというくらいに、自発的であることが忘れ去られるきらいがある。ところがぼくたち大人が子供だった頃は、遊びながら何通りもの階段の使いみちを発見したものだ。ぼくは階段を上り、寝室へ向かった。この家の寝室ならば、きっと星空の下で寝ている気分になるだろう。そう思えるのは大きな窓のせいだろうか。それとも部屋の雰囲気なのか。あるいは部屋の中央に小さな柱があるせいだろうか。たぶんそのすべてが影響しているのだろう。2階の見どころといえば、この家の女主人が使うアトリエである。そこには中庭に面して大きな窓が並ぶ。この部屋は、家の中と外の様子を把握するには格好の位置にある。つまりここは家の最上部にあたる。この部分は木製のファサードになっていることから、全体のマッスにおけるアクセントになっている。この点で、今の人たちは数々の写真を通じて馴染みがあるはずだ。アトリエのロフト部分はギャラリーになっており、そのための船舶用の梯子が架けられている。ギャラリーでぼくが見つけたのは、山積みになった古い麦藁帽子だ。

ぼくたちは下の階に戻った。広々としたキッチンは居心地が良いので、つい食堂へ行かずにここで長話をするはめになる。林の眺めも清々しい。食堂の突き当たりには出口があり、その外には面白い格好をしたキャノピーが張り出し、スレート積みの暖炉もある。暖炉の脇の階段を上ると、屋上テラスに出る。サウナへのアクセスは風習どおり、屋外からだ。キャノピーもテラスもプールに面しているサウナは、サマー・コテージにあるような飾り気のないサウナを彷彿させる。フリー・フォームのプールの場合は、森の中の小さな池と似ている。前回訪れたときにはここで泳いだが、その際ぼくはプールの底もフリー・フォームであることに気がついた。

日が沈み始めた。ぼくらは中庭から家の中を通り抜けることにした。壁に飾られた何点もの美しい絵画に、ぼくは目をとめた。この家からは、住み手のハリーとマイレ・グリクセンの思いがひしひしと伝わってくる。夫妻の価値観、ライフスタイル、そして哲学が表われている。このヴィラ・マイレアのように、偏見にとらわれることのないリベラルな施主と、名建築家とが手を組むことなど、もちろん例外的にしか起こり得ない。その帰結として生まれたのが総合芸術（ゲザムトクンストヴェルク）、すなわち施主と建築家とが共同でつくり上げた作品である。人と自然、また伝統と近代の生活様式には、幸福な結婚もあるのだという希望は、このヴィラ・マイレアで叶えられた。この建物には現実離れしたところがあるにせよ、フィンランドのごく普通の家とそっくりなところもある。アアルトにしろグリクセン夫妻にしろ、そろって社会改良主義家であった。そしてヴィラ・マイレアには、より良い世界とはどのようなものかが示された。

アアルトとヴィラ・マイレアの女主人は親しい間柄で、ときには親密になりすぎることさえあった。かつて歴史家のジークフリート・ギーディオンがこの家を訪れたことがある。彼はこの家がそれまで自分が綴ってきたアアルト寄りの主張に反するものであると悟った。そしてアアルトに言った。「君がつくったのは建物じゃない。一編の恋愛詩だよ」と。

ふたたび機上から

ぼくたちの旅は終わった。ぼくらは空港で別れの言葉を交わした。ヤリはクンプラの自宅に帰った。ミエは東京行きの便で飛び立って行った。その機首にはムーミンの絵がついていた。ぼくはロンドン行きの飛行機の中にいる。こちらの機首にはサンタ・クロースの絵が描かれている。旅の間はじつに中身の濃い1週間であった。ぼくは、いつとはなしに旅の後の物想いに沈んでしまった。小さな窓の外に目をやった。湖や川が曲がりくねっている。アアルトがつくった住宅のようだ。

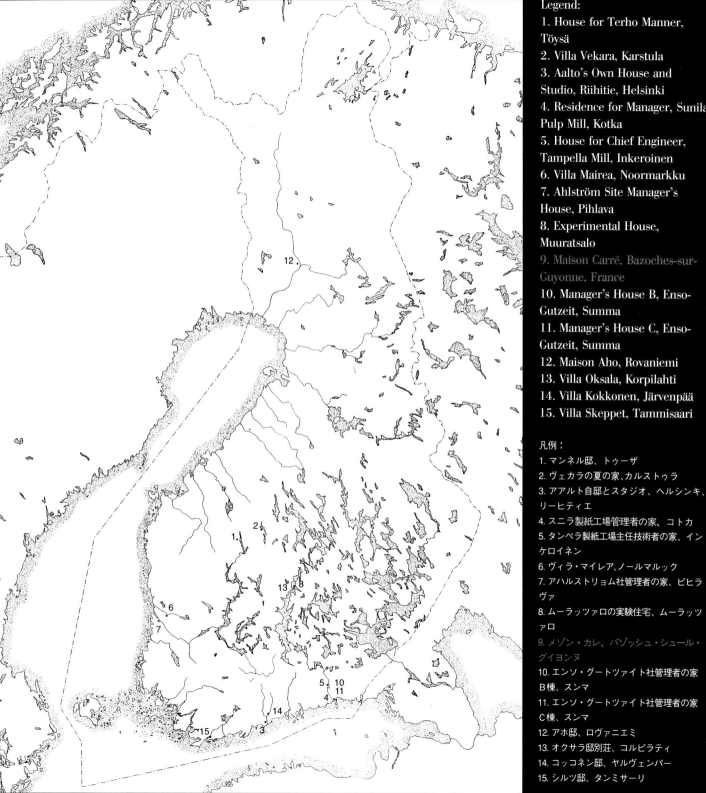

Legend:
1. House for Terho Manner, Töysä
2. Villa Vekara, Karstula
3. Aalto's Own House and Studio, Riihitie, Helsinki
4. Residence for Manager, Sunila Pulp Mill, Kotka
5. House for Chief Engineer, Tampella Mill, Inkeroinen
6. Villa Mairea, Noormarkku
7. Ahlström Site Manager's House, Pihlava
8. Experimental House, Muuratsalo
9. Maison Carré, Bazoches-sur-Guyonne, France
10. Manager's House B, Enso-Gutzeit, Summa
11. Manager's House C, Enso-Gutzeit, Summa
12. Maison Aho, Rovaniemi
13. Villa Oksala, Korpilahti
14. Villa Kokkonen, Järvenpää
15. Villa Skeppet, Tammisaari

凡例：
1. マンネル邸、トゥーザ
2. ヴェカラの夏の家、カルストゥラ
3. アアルト自邸とスタジオ、ヘルシンキ、リーヒティエ
4. スニラ製紙工場管理者の家、コトカ
5. タンペラ製紙工場主任技術者の家、インケロイネン
6. ヴィラ・マイレア、ノールマルック
7. アハルストリョム社管理者の家、ピヒラヴァ
8. ムーラッツァロの実験住宅、ムーラッツァロ
9. メゾン・カレ、バゾッシュ・シュール・グイヨンヌ
10. エンソ・グートツァイト社管理者の家 B棟、スンマ
11. エンソ・グートツァイト社管理者の家 C棟、スンマ
12. アホ邸、ロヴァニエミ
13. オクサラ邸別荘、コルピラティ
14. コッコネン邸、ヤルヴェンパー
15. シルツ邸、タンミサーリ

Chronology 年表

1898

- 1898 Born in Kuortane, Finland on February 3
- 1916 Commencement of study in architecture, Helsinki University of Technology under Professors Usko Nyström and Armas Lindgren
- 1917 Declaration of independence of Finland. Aalto took part in the War of Independence
- 1919 Alajärvi Youth Association building (later becomes the Civil Guard Building)*
- 1920 Elementary school for Kauhajärvi
- 1921 Received Diploma of Architecture from Helsinki University of Technology under Professor Sigurd Frosterus
  Worked for Arvid Bjerke in Gothenberg, Sweden
  Toured in several Baltic and Scandinavian countries on a Finnish government scholarship
  Kauhajärvi bell tower and church*
- 1922 Second Finnish trade fair in Tampere*
- 1923 Established The Alvar Aalto Office for Architecture and Monumental Art in Jyväskylä
  Introduced to Erik Gunnar Asplund in Stockholm
  Restoration of Toivakka Church*
  Chief Constable Karpio's summer villa, Jyväskylä*
  Nuora House, Jyväskylä*
  House for Terho Manner, Töysä*
  Competition entry, Finnish Parliament House
- 1924 Married to Aino Marsio who worked in partnership with him. She died in 1949
  Alajärvi Municipal Hospital*
  Seinäjoki Defence Corps Building*
  Jyväskylä Workers' Club*
  Railway officials' block of flats, Jyväskylä*
  Furnishing of the Seurahuone Cafe, Jyväskylä*
  Villa Vekara, Karstula*
- 1925 Renovation of Kemijärvi Church*
  Renovation of Korpilahti Church*
  Pertunmaa Church
  Funeral Chapel for Jyväskylä
  Competition entry, Jämsä Church
  Perniö Museum
  "Casa Laurén", Jyväskylä*
  "Atrium House" for Väinö Aalto, Alajärvi
- 1926 Competition entry, Jyväskylä vicarage
  Jyväskylä Defence Corps Building*
  Competition entry, Union Bank Building, Helsinki
  "Villa Flora", Alajärvi*
  Town plan for Sammallahti, Jämsä municipality
  Sketches, Palais de Nations, Geneva, Switzerland
  Muurame Church, Muurame*
- 1927 Moved architectural office to Turku
  Officials' housing, Wilh. Schauman Co. Joensuu*
  Competition entry, health spa in Pärnu, Estonia
  Competition entry, Viipuri City Library (now in Vyborg, Russia)*
  Competition entry, Töölö Church, Helsinki
  Competition entry, Southwest Finland Agricultural Coop. Building, Turku*
  Competition entry, Taulumäki Church, Jyväskylä
  Competition entry, Viinikka Church, Tampere
  Competition entry, Kinkomaa Tuberculosis Sanatorium
  "Standard apartment block", the Tapani Building, Turku*
- 1928 Became permanent member of the Congrès Internationaux d'Architecture Moderne
  Introduced to Henningsen in Denmark and Alfred Roth in Paris

1930

  Suomen Biografi Cinema, Turku
  Turun Sanomat Building, Turku*
  Three houses, Aitta Summer House competition*
  Competition entry, Paimio Tuberculosis Sanatorium*
  Competition entry, Independence Monument, Helsinki
  Competition entry for a lighthouse, Dominican Republic
  Furniture developed with Otto Korhonen*
- 1929 Attended CIAM in Frankfurt. Introduced to László Moholy-Nagy, Walter Gropius, Le Corbusier, Karl Moser, Sigfried Giedion
  Competition entry, Kälviä Tuberculosis Sanatorium
  Competition entry, Vallila Church, Helsinki
  City of Turku 700th Anniversary Exhibition*
- 1930 Attended CIAM in Brussels with a presentation of Finnish modern design
  Toppila-Vaara pulp mill, Oulu*
  Competition entry, Turku water tower
  Competition entry, Vierumäki Sports Institute
  Competition entry, Tehtaanpuisto Church, Helsinki
  Competition entry, G.A. Serlachius Company headquarters, Mänttä
  Sets for pacifist play at Turku Finnish Theatre*
  Furnishing of living room, bedroom, and kitchen at the "Rationalization of the Minimum Dwelling" Exhibition, Helsinki Art Hall*
- 1931 Competition entry, enlargement of the University of Helsinki
  Competition entry, Zagreb Central Hospital, Yugoslavia
  Competition entries, Lallukka artists' home,

1

- 1898 2月3日フィンランド、クオルタネに生まれる
- 1916 ヘルシンキ工科大学建築学科入学。当時の教授はウスコ・ニシュトロムとアルマス・リンドグレン
- 1917 フィンランド独立宣言。アアルト、独立戦争に参加
- 1919 アラヤルヴィ青年館（自衛団ビルとなる）*
- 1920 カウハヤルヴィ小学校*
- 1921 シーグルト・フロステルスの教育を受け、ヘルシンキ工科大学建築学科卒業
  アルヴィド・ビエルケ事務所で働く、スウェーデン、ゲーテボルグ
  フィンランド政府の奨学金でバルト海、スカンディナヴィア地方を研修旅行する
  教会と鐘楼、カウハヤルヴィ*
- 1922 産業展示場、タンペレ*
- 1923 ユヴァスキュラに設計事務所を設立
  ストックホルムでエリック・グンナー・アスプルンドと出会う
  トイヴァッカ教会の改修*
  ヴィラ・カルピオ、ユヴァスキュラ*
  ヌオラ・ハウス、ユヴァスキュラ*
  マンネル邸、トゥーザ*
  国会議事堂、ヘルシンキ（コンペ）
- 1924 アイノ・マルシオ（1949年没）と結婚。設計事務所で共同して仕事を始める
  市立病院、アラヤルヴィ*
  自衛団ビル、セイナヨキ*
  労働者会館、ユヴァスキュラ*
  鉄道職員のためのアパートメント、ユヴァスキュラ*
  セウラホネ・カフェの内装、ユヴァスキュラ*
  ヴェカラの夏の家、カルストゥラ*
- 1925 ケミヤルヴィ教会の修復*
  コルピラティ教会の修復*
  ペルトゥンマ教会
  葬儀場、ユヴァスキュラ
  ヤムサ教会（コンペ）
  ペルニオ博物館
  「カーサ・ローレン」、ユヴァスキュラ*
  弟ヴァイノ・アアルトのための「アトリウム・ハウス」、アラヤルヴィ
- 1926 ユヴァスキュラ教区牧師の住居（コンペ）
  自衛団ビル、ユヴァスキュラ*
  ユニオン銀行（コンペ）
  「ヴィラ・フローラ」、アラヤルヴィ*
  サンマラティ都市計画、ヤムサ
  国際連盟本部、スイス、ジュネーヴ（コンペ）
  ムーラメ教会、ムーラメ
- 1927 設計事務所をトゥルクに移す
  シャウマン社職員の住宅、ヨエンスー*
  ペルヌの温泉スパ、エストニア（コンペ）
  ヴィープリ市立図書館（コンペ）*
  トーロ教会、ヘルシンキ（コンペ）
  南西農業協同組合ビル、トゥルク（コンペ）*
  タウルマキ教会、ユヴァスキュラ（コンペ）
  ヴィーニッカ教会、タンペレ（コンペ）
  キンコマ・サナトリウム（コンペ）
  タパニ・ビル規格住宅、トゥルク*
- 1928 CIAMの終身会員となる
  デンマークでヘニングセンに、そしてパリでアルフレッド・ロートに出会う
  スオメン・ビオグラフィ映画館、トゥルク
  トゥルン・サノマト新聞社、トゥルク*
  『アイッタ』誌主催のサマーハウス（コンペ）*
  パイミオ・サナトリウム（コンペ）*
  独立記念碑、ヘルシンキ（コンペ）
  灯台、ドミニカ共和国（コンペ）
  家具（オット・コルホネンとの共同デザイン）*
- 1929 フランクフルトで開かれたCIAMに参加する。ラズロ・モホリ＝ナギ、ヴァルター・グロピウス、ル・コルビュジエ、カール・モーザーとジークフリード・ギーディオンに出会う
  カルヴィア・サナトリウム（コンペ）
  ヴァッリラ教会、ヘルシンキ（コンペ）
  トゥルク市700年祭博覧会*
- 1930 ブリュッセルで開かれたCIAMに参加し、フィンランドのモダン・デザインを紹介する
  トッピラ・ヴァーラのセルロース工場、オウル*
  給水塔、トゥルク（コンペ）
  ヴィエルマキ体育研究所（コンペ）
  テヘターンプイスト教会、ヘルシンキ（コンペ）
  G・A・セラキウス社のマンタ本社（コンペ）
  平和主義的演劇のステージ・デザイン、トゥルク・フィンランド劇場*
  居間、寝室、台所の内装、「最小限住宅」展、ヘルシンキ・アート・ホール*
- 1931 ヘルシンキ大学増築（コンペ）
  ザグレブ中央病院（コンペ）
  ラルッカ芸術家の集合住宅（コンペ）
- 1932 扇形サウナ、パイミオ*
  エンソ・グートツァイト社の週末別荘（コンペ）
  タンメカン邸、エストニア、タルトゥ*
  イッタラ社主催実用ガラス製品コンペ*
- 1933 設計事務所をヘルシンキに移す
  アテネで開かれたCIAMに参加。フェルナン・レジェ、

1940

	Helsinki		Master plan and housing for Varkaus*		on the problem of reconstruction at MIT. Visited Edgar Kaufmann, Jr. at Fallingwater, in Pennsylvania, designed by Frank Lloyd Wright

1932 Fan-shaped sauna, Paimio*
Competition entry, Enso-Gutzeit weekend cottage
Villa Tammekann, Tartu, Estonia*
Karhula-Iittala Glass Design competition*
1933 Moved architectural office to Helsinki
Attended CIAM in Athens. Introduced to Fernand Léger, José Luis Sert, Pierre Jeanneret
Entry in the ideas competition for Nedre Norrmalm, Stockholm
Competition entry, Temppeliaukio Church, Helsinki
Entry in the first competition, Helsinki Stadium
Entry in the final competition, Helsinki Stadium
Viipuri City Library, final version*
1934 Founded Projektio, Finland's first film society
Competition entry, Helsinki Fair Hall
Competition entry, Tampere railway station
Competition entry, Helsinki Main Post Office
Aalto's own house and studio, Helsinki*
Town plan for Munkkiniemi, Helsinki
High-rise housing area in Munkkiniemi, Helsinki
1935 Founded Artek (a furniture company) with Maire Gullichsen and others
Address at the annual meeting of the Swedish Craft Society: "Rationalism and Man"
Kalastajatorppa restaurant, Helsinki
Competition entry, Finnish Embassy, Moscow, Russia
1936 Competition entry, central warehouse of the State Alcohol Monopoly, Helsinki
Competition entry, Finnish Pavilion, 1937 World's Fair in Paris*
Karhula-Iittala Glass Design competition*

Master plan and housing for Varkaus*
Master plan, pulp mill, and housing for Sunila, Kotka*
1937 Introduced to Pablo Picasso, Alexander Calder, Constantin Brancusi, Christian Zervos
Competition entry, extension to Helsinki University Library
Competition entry, Tallinn Art Museum, Estonia
Villa Mairea, Noormarkku*
Master plan and housing for Karhula*
Nordic Union Bank branch office in Karhula*
Master plan, paper mill, and housing for Tampella Mill, Inkeroinen*
Weekend house for Mr. Richmond Temple
Furnishing of the Savoy restaurant in Helsinki*
A-House Standard Houses*
1938 Exhibition at the Museum of Modern Art in New York: "Alvar Aalto: Architecture and Furniture"*
Address at the Nordic Building Conference, Oslo: "The Influence of Construction and Materials on Modern Architecture"
Master plan and housing for Kauttua*
Inkeroinen Elementary School*
Three competition entries, Finnish Pavilion, 1939 World's Fair in New York*
"Forest pavilion", Agricultural Exhibition at Lapua*
Film studio for Erik Blomberg in Westend, Espoo
Jalasjärvi Defence Corps building
1939–40 War with USSR (The Winter War)
1939 Introduced to Marcel Breuer
1940 Journey to the USA with an exhibition on the destruction caused by the war in Finland and on the activity of the Finnish Red Cross. Researched

on the problem of reconstruction at MIT. Visited Edgar Kaufmann, Jr. at Fallingwater, in Pennsylvania, designed by Frank Lloyd Wright
HAKA (Helsinki Housing Association) housing competition in Helsinki
"An American town in Finland"
AA System standardized houses*
"Village of comrades in arms" in Tampere*
1941–44 War with USSR (The Continuation War)
1941 Address at ETH Zürich: "Problems of Reconstruction in Europe"
Regional plan for the Kokemäenjoki river valley*
A. Ahlström Company head office in Varkaus
Entrance to bomb shelter at Erottaja, Helsinki*
1942 Master plan and low-rise housing for Säynätsalo*
Competition entry for Merikoski power plant, Oulu
Villa Tvistbo near Ludvika, Sweden
1943–58 Served as chairman of the Association of Finnish Architects (Honorary member since 1958)
1943 Town plan, "River Rapids Centre", Oulu
Master plan for the Strömberg company's industrial estate and housing in Vaasa*
Master plan for Nynäshamn, Sweden*
1944 Johnson Institute in Avesta, Sweden
Town centre of Avesta
"Reindeer horn plan" for Rovaniemi*
Sauna in Kauttua*
1945 Addresses in Amsterdam: "Reconstruction in Northern Finland"
Competition entry for Nynäshamn Town Hall
1946–48 Visiting professor at MIT
1946 Visited Frank Lloyd Wright in Milwaukee and Spring Green, Wisconsin

2

ホセ・ルイ・セルト、ピエール・ジャンヌレに出会う
ノッルマルム再開発計画、ストックホルム（コンペ）
テンペリアウキオ教会、ヘルシンキ（コンペ）
ヘルシンキ・スタジアム、初回コンペ案
ヘルシンキ・スタジアム、最終コンペ案
ヴィープリ市立図書館、最終案＊
1934 フィンランド初の映画組織プロジェクティオを設立
ヘルシンキ展示会館（コンペ）
鉄道駅舎、タンペレ（コンペ）
ヘルシンキ中央郵便局（コンペ）
アアルト自邸とスタジオ、ヘルシンキ＊
ムンクニエミ都市計画、ヘルシンキ
高層住宅地区、ヘルシンキ、ムンクニエミ
1935 マイレ・グリクセンほか数人で家具会社アルテクを設立
スウェーデン工芸家協会、年次総会で講演「合理主義と人間」
カラスタヤトルパ・レストラン、ヘルシンキ
フィンランド大使館、モスクワ（コンペ）
1936 国営酒類専売公社の製造工場とオフィス、ヘルシンキ（コンペ）
パリ万国博フィンランド館（コンペ）＊
イッタラ社主催実用ガラス製品コンペ＊
ヴァルカウス都市計画、住宅＊
スニラ総合計画、セルロース工場、住宅地区、コトカ＊
1937 パブロ・ピカソ、アレクサンダー・カルダー、コンスタンティン・ブランクージ、クリスチャン・ゼルヴォに出会う
ヘルシンキ大学図書館増築（コンペ）
タリン美術館、エストニア（コンペ）
ヴィラ・マイレア、ノールマルック＊

カルフラ総合計画、住宅＊
ノルディック・ユニオン銀行、カルフラ＊
タンペラ社周辺の総合計画、製紙工場、住宅、インケロイネン＊
リッチモンド・テンプル氏の週末別荘
サヴォイ・レストラン内装、ヘルシンキ＊
A-HOUSE規格住宅＊
1938 アアルト「建築と家具」展、ニューヨーク近代美術館（MoMA）＊
オスロで開かれた北欧建築会議で講演、「工法および材料の近代建築への影響」
カウットゥア総合計画、住宅＊
インケロイネン小学校＊
ニューヨーク万国博フィンランド館（コンペ）＊
「林業館」、ラプア農業博覧会＊
エリック・ブロンベリの映画製作所、エスポー
自衛団ビル、ヤラスヤルヴィ
1939〜40 フィンランドはソ連と交戦（冬の戦争）
1939 マルセル・ブロイヤーと出会う
1940 アメリカへ渡り、戦争の爪跡と赤十字の活動を報告
マサチューセッツ工科大学で戦後の再建の問題を研究
エドガー・カウフマン・ジュニアに会うためフランク・ロイド・ライト設計の「落水荘」を訪れる
HAKA（ヘルシンキ住宅協会）集合住居計画、ヘルシンキ
「アメリカン・タウン・イン・フィンランド」
AAシステム規格住宅＊
「戦友の村」、タンペレ＊
1941〜44 再びソ連と交戦（第2次世界大戦）
1941 チューリッヒのスイス連邦工科大学で講演、「ヨーロッパ再建」

コケマエンヨキ谷の地域計画＊
アハルストリョム本社ビル、ヴァルカウス
エロッタヤ防空シェルター入口、ヘルシンキ＊
1942 セイナッツァロ総合計画、住宅＊
メリコスキ発電所、オウル（コンペ）
ヴィラ・ツヴィスボ、スウェーデン、ルドヴィカ近郊
1943〜58 フィンランド建築家協会の会長を務める。1958年以降、名誉会員となる
1943 オウル川辺計画、「リヴァー・ラピッド・センター」
ストリョムベルグ社集合住居計画、ヴァーサ＊
ニュネスハムン総合計画、スウェーデン＊
1944 ジョンソン・リサーチ・インスティテュート、スウェーデン、アヴェスタ
アヴェスタ・タウン・センター、スウェーデン
「トナカイの角」計画、ロヴァニエミ＊
サウナ、カウットゥア＊
1945 アムステルダムで講演、「北フィンランドの再建」
ニュネスハムンの役場、スウェーデン（コンペ）
1946〜48 米国、マサチューセッツ工科大学、客員教授を務める
1946 フランク・ロイド・ライトに会うためウィスコンシン州、ミルウォーキーとスプリング・グリーンを訪れる
アルテク展示館、スウェーデン、ヘデモラ＊
ハイムダル集合住居、スウェーデン、ニュネスハムン
ヴィラ・カウッピ、ヘイノラ近郊、ヒルヴィサロ＊
ベーカー・ハウス寄宿舎、米国、マサチューセッツ工科大学
アハルストリョム社管理者の家、ピヒラヴァ＊
1947 アイノ＆アルヴァ・アアルト、共同設計25周年記念展、ヘルシンキ＊
イマトラ総合計画＊

1950

	Artek pavilion in Hedemora, Sweden*
	Heimdal housing area in Nynäshamn, Sweden
	Villa Kauppi in Hirvisalo near Heinola*
	Baker House, MIT, Cambridge, Massachusetts*
	House for site manager, Ahlström Company, Pihlava*
1947	Aino and Alvar Aalto exhibition in Helsinki, celebrating 25 years of collaboration*
	Master plan of Imatra*
	Villa Kihlman on Lake Näsijärvi*
1948	Competition entry, National Pensions Institute, Helsinki*
	Finnish Engineering Society building, Helsinki*
	Competition entry, Säynätsalo Town Hall*
1949	Town planning competition for Otaniemi, Espoo*
	Competition entry, passenger terminal, Helsinki*
	Plans for Helsinki University of Technology, Espoo. The university was destroyed in 1939*
1950	Regional plan for the province of Lapland
	Indoor stadium, Otaniemi Campus, Espoo*
	Competition entry, Lahti Church
	Competition entry, chapel in Malmi graveyard, Helsinki
	Competition entry, Kivelä Hospital in Helsinki
1951	Area plan, factory, and housing for Typpi Company, Oulu*
	Competition entry for Seinäjoki Church*
	Competition entry for Glostrup Hospital, Copenhagen, Denmark
	Competition entry for Jyväskylä Institute of Pedagogics (later Jyväskylä University)*
	"Rautatalo" (Iron house) commercial building in Helsinki*
	Country club for Enso-Gutzeit, Kallahti, Helsinki*
1952	Married to Elissa Mäkiniemi
	Competition entry, funeral chapel and cemetery in Lyngby-Taarbaek, Denmark
	Competition entry, Kuopio Theatre
	National Pensions Institute office in Helsinki*
	Experimental House on Muuratsalo Island*
	House of Culture, Helsinki*
1953	Helsinki University of Technology main building*
	National Pensions Institute housing in Helsinki*
	Competition entry, sports/concerts complex at Vogelweidplatz, Vienna, Austria
1954	Master plan, paper mill, and housing for Enso-Gutzeit Company in Summa*
	Alvar Aalto's studio in Munkkiniemi, Helsinki*
	Apartment block, Hansaviertel, Berlin, Germany*
	Central Finland Museum in Jyväskylä*
	The motor boat "Nemo propheta in patria"*
1955	Became member of the Finnish Academy. Address upon his membership: "Art and Technology"
	Address at the Central Union of Architects in Vienna: "Between Humanism and Materialism"
	Villa Sambonet in a Milan suburb, Italy
	Competition entry, National Bank head office, Baghdad, Iraq
	Theatre and concert hall in Oulu
	Competition entry, municipal offices in Gothenburg, Sweden
	Finnish Pavilion, Venice's Biennale park, Italy*
	Church of the Three Crosses at Vuoksenniska, Imatra*
	Housing and business complex "Sundh Center" in Avesta, Sweden*
	Typpi Company site manager's house "Villa Lehmus" in Oulu*
1956	Competition entry, main railway station in Gothenburg, Sweden
	Maison Carré, Bazoches-sur-Guyonne, France*
	Korkalovaara housing area in Rovaniemi*
	Plan for University of Oulu campus
1957	Address upon receiving the Royal Institute of British Architects Gold Medal: "The Architectural Struggle"
	Address at a Swedish city planners' meeting in Malmö: "The Architect's Conception of Paradise"
	Town plan/housing, Kampementsbacken, Stockholm
	Competition entry, Marl Town Hall, Germany
	Art Museum in Baghdad, Iraq
	General Post Office in Baghdad, Iraq
1958	Address for Jyväskylä Lycée Hundred Year Jubilee
	Wolfsburg Cultural Centre, Germany*
	North Jutland Art Museum in Aalborg, Denmark*
	Competition entry for Kiruna Town Hall, Sweden
	Seinäjoki Town Hall*
	"Neue Vahr" high-rise apartment building, Bremen, Germany*
	Munkkiniemi youth centre, Helsinki
1959	Opera house and music theatre, Essen, Germany*
	Town plan and housing for Karhusaari and Hanasaari islands, Espoo
	Enso-Gutzeit Company headquarters, Helsinki*
	Managers' houses for Enso-Gutzeit, Summa*
	Plans for the new centre of Helsinki
	Memorial to the Battle of Suomussalmi, sculpture*
	Power plant at the Lieksankoski rapids
1960	Received honorary doctorate from the Norwegian Institute of Technology at Trondheim. Address at

3

1960

       the reception: "The Current Problems in Architecture and in the Fine Arts"
       Enlargement of the Nordic Union Bank head office, Helsinki*
       Church centre in Wolfsburg, Germany*
       Competition entry, cultural centre in Leverkusen, Germany
       Shopping centre in Otaniemi, Espoo*
       Power plant at the Pankakoski rapids*
       Seinäjoki City Library*
1961 Rovaniemi administrative and cultural centre*
       Seinäjoki City Theatre*
       Apartment blocks in Tapiola, Espoo*
       Extension to Stockmann Department Store, Helsinki*
       Academic Bookshop, Helsinki*
       Institute of International Education, New York*
       Västmanland-Dala student building in Uppsala, Sweden*
1962 Received the Sonning Prize, Denmark
       Finlandia Hall, Helsinki*
       Competition entry, extension to Enskilda Bank head office, Stockholm, Sweden
       Scandinavian House in Reykjavik, Iceland*
       Institute of Physical Education, University of Jyväskylä*
1963–68 President of the Finnish Academy (Emeritus member since 1968)
1963 Received the Gold Medal from the American Institute of Architecture
       Church centre in Detmerode, Germany*
       Row house in Jakobstad*
       Student housing, Helsinki University of Technology*
1964 Jyväskylä administrative and cultural centre*
       Master plan for Kivenlahti-Soukka, Espoo
       Competition entry, British Petroleum administrative building, Hamburg, Germany
       Competition entry, Pohjola Insurance Company head office in Helsinki
       Schönbühl high-rise apartments, Lucerne, Switzerland*
       Office building, Seinäjoki*
       Maison Aho, Rovaniemi*
       Ekenäs Savings Bank, Ekenäs*
       Helsinki University of Technology Library*
1965 William Lehtinen Museum in Helsinki
       Administrative building, Helsinki City Power Company, Helsinki*
       Church centre, Riola, Italy*
       Urban centre, Castrop-Rauxel, Germany
       Alajärvi Town Hall*
       Mount Angel Benedictine Abbey Library, Oregon, USA*
       Enlargement of the Jyväskylä University gymnasium building*
       Villa Oksala on Ruotsula Island, Korpilahti*
1966 Comprehensive exhibition of Aalto's works in Palazzo Strozzi, Florence, Italy*
       Address at the Finnish Architectural Association's Congress for Planning of Greater Helsinki: "Town Planning and Public Buildings"
       Concert hall, Siena, Italy
       Competition entry, theatre in Wolfsburg, Germany
       Housing for Gammelbacka, Porvoo municipality
       Patricia suburb of Pavia, Italy

1976

1967 Competition entry, church centre in Zürich-Alstetten, Switzerland
       Jyväskylä police headquarters*
       Villa Kokkonen, Järvenpää*
1968 Water tower, Helsinki University of Technology*
1969 Became member of Pour le Mérite in Germany
       Lappia multipurpose building, Rovaniemi*
       Museum of Modern Art in Shiraz, Iran
       Main church of Lahti*
       Villa Skeppet (for Göran Schildt), Tammisaari*
       Villa Erica, Monsalieri near Turin, Italy
1971 Alvar Aalto Museum in Jyväskylä*
1972 Received the Gold Medal from the French Academy of Architecture
1973 Exhibition at the Finnish Museum for Modern Architecture: "Alvar Aalto — Sketches"*
       The Midwest Institute of Scandinavian Culture, Wisconsin, USA
1974 Health spa in Reykjavik, Iceland
1975 Plan for the University of Reykjavik area, Iceland
1976 Died in Helsinki on May 11

Year indicates start of project.   * partly or fully realized

1: Paimio Tuberculosis Sanatorium
2: Säynätsalo Town Hall
3: Helsinki University of Technology
4: Finlandia Hall
1, 3, 4 ©Shinkenchiku-sha
2 ©Kanji Hayashi

4

Biography of Writers and Photographer

著者・写真家・翻訳者略歴

Markku Ilmari Lahti
Born in Jyväskylä, Finland in 1947. Received his BA (1970) and MA (1971) from Jyväskylä University. Exhibition secretary of Alvar Aalto Museum (1972). Director of Alvar Aalto Museum since 1973. He has been a member of National Centenary Committee of Alvar Aalto and representative of the Finnish Academy in the board of the Alvar Aalto Foundation since 1995.
His books include *Museologian Perusteet (Handbook on Museology)*, 1988, joint work with Jouko Heinonen, *Suomalaisen Taideopas (Finnish Art Guide)*, 1989, joint work with Louna Lahti and *Alvar Aalto, A Gentler Structure for Life*, 1998, joint work with Maija Holma (photos).

Matti Sanaksenaho
Born in Helsinki, Finland, 1966. Received his MA from Helsinki University of Technology, 1993. During his school days he and four other students established the architectural office Monark (1990-1992) and took 1st prize in the Finnish Pavilion competition of Expo 92, Seville. Established his own office in 1992; since 1997 collaboration with Pirjo Sanaksenaho.
Major works include: Chapel "Empty Space" for Tapper Foundation in Saarijärvi, 1992-1993; Student center, Vaasa, 1993-1997; Santapark, Rovaniemi, 1997-.

Jari Tapani Jetsonen
Born in Hämeenlinna, Finland in 1958. Graduated from Kouvolan Drawing School in 1978. While working at architectural offices of Into Pyykkö, Helsinki (1979-1982) and Gullichsen-Kairamo-Vormala Ky (1981) he set up his own firm Pienoismallit Jari Jetsonen Oy in 1980. Artisan, artist and photographer.
His major works include: models of Säynätsalo Town Hall, Villa Mairea, and Paimio Sanatorium for Alvar Aalto Museum; photographs for the book of Reima and Raili Pietilä, Tango/ Mäntyniemi, 1994.
Since 1986 he has taught at Helsinki University of Technology, Faculty of Architecture, information course. Organized many architectural exhibitions around the world.

マルック・ラティ
1947年、フィンランド、ユヴァスキュラに生まれる。ユヴァスキュラ大学にて学士号（1970）、修士号（1971）を取得。1972年にはアルヴァ・アアルト美術館にて学芸員を、1973年より同美術館の館長を務め現在にいたる。また、1995年よりアルヴァ・アアルト生誕100年国民記念委員会メンバー、アルヴァ・アアルト財団委員会のフィンランド・アカデミー代表。著書には『博物館学のハンドブック（1988年刊）』、『フィンランド芸術の案内（1989年刊）』、『アルヴァ・アアルト　生活のための上質の建築（1998年刊）』などがある。

マッティ・サナクセンアホ
1966年、フィンランド、ヘルシンキ生まれ。ヘルシンキ工科大学にて1993年修士号を取得。在学中に他4人の学生とともにモナーク（1990〜1992）を結成し、セヴィリア万博フィンランド館のコンペで一等となる。1992年にヘルシンキに事務所を開き独立。1997年より夫人のピーリョ・サナクセンアホと共同。
代表作にはエンプティ・スペース（サーリヤルヴィ、1992〜1994）、ヴァーサの学生寮（1993〜1997）、サンタパーク（ロヴァニエミ、1997〜）などがある。

ヤリ・タパニ・イエッツオネン
1958年、フィンランド、ハーメンリンナに生まれる。イント・ピッコやグリクセン－カイラモ－ヴォルマラの建築設計事務所に勤務する傍ら、1980年模型制作会社を設立。主な作品は、アルヴァ・アアルト美術館のために制作したセイナッツァロの役場、ヴィラ・マイレア、パイミオのサナトリウムなどの模型があり、また、写真家としてレイマ・アンド・ライリ・ピエティラの作品集を刊行している。1986年からはヘルシンキ工科大学建築学科で教鞭を執ったり、各国での建築に関する展覧会を企画するなど幅広く活動している。

田中雅美
1954年、東京生まれ。1979年に日本大学で修士号を取得後1981年まで土岐新建築総合計画事務所に勤務。1981年から1986年、フィンランドのカルロ・レッパネン建築事務所に勤務。1989年、東京にシサピハ建築事務所（現田中雅美建築設計事務所）を設立。訳書には『白い机－アルヴァ・アアルト若い時（鹿島出版会）』、『白い机－モダン・タイムス（鹿島出版会）』などがある。

Credits and Acknowledgements

クレジット・謝辞

Photographs:
Jari Jetsonen:
Cover, back cover, pp. 25-80, pp.103-164, pp.167-196, pp.215-223, p.232; photos of drawings on p.44, p.81, 212
Antti Bengts: p.1
M. Kapanen: p.9, p.10 top and bottom, p.13
Turun Sanomat: p.14
Markku Lahti: p.16
Shinkenchiku-sha: p.226, 228, 229
Kanji Hayashi: 227

Drawings:
All drawings courtesy of Alvar Aalto Foundation
(Site plans on p.24, p.30, p.52, p.102, p.135, p.166, p.174 were newly drawn with the cooperation of Vilhelm Helander, Juha Leiviskä Arkkitehdit SAFA)

Descriptions:
Markku Lahti, Director, Alvar Aalto Museum

English translation from Finnish:
Nicholas Mayow, English Center: "Alvar Aalto's One-family Houses: Paradises for Ordinary People" by Markku Lahti, all descriptions
Laura Mänki, Valtasana Ltd: "Visiting the Houses of Aalto" by Matti Sanaksenaho

English translation from Japanese:
Thomas Donahue: Editor's Foreword

Japanese translation:
Masami Tanaka: " Alvar Aalto's One-family Houses: Paradises for Ordinary People" by Markku Lahti
Jun Doi: "Visiting the Houses of Aalto" by Matti Sanaksenaho
A+U Editorial Dept: All descriptions

Alvar Aalto Houses: Timeless Expressions could not have been published without the encouraging cooperation of Alvar Aalto Foundation, Alvar Aalto Museum and Jari Jetsonen, photographer. We would like to extend special thanks to the following people.
Owners of Aalto houses: Joonas and Anita Kokkonen, Göran Schildt, Olga Carré, Rauni Aho, Eeva-Marjatta Karstu, Kristiina and Markus Korte, Jaakko and Marjaleena Lahti, Hanni Alanen, Olavi and Sirpa Airanne, Antti Aho, Pellervo and Tarkko Oksala and Johanna Pakoma.
Owner companies of Aalto houses and contact persons: Anna Hahl, Ahlström; Marjaliisa Uski, Enso Group, Summa Factory; Aarno Sihvola, Enso Group, Inkeroinen; Päivi Tötterman, Sunila Oy.
Drawer of new site plans: Masaaki Takahashi, Vilhelm Helander, Juha Leiviskä Arkkitehdit SAFA.
Cooperation with research in the Aalto archives: Mia Hipeli, Alvar Aalto Foundation and Sabine Kraenker, Helsinki University of Technology.
Additionally, we would also like to thank Sirkkaliisa Jetsonen, architect and researcher of Helsinki Institute of Technology, Matti and Pirjo Sanaksenaho, architects, and Hanni Sippo, Alvar Aalto Museum, who accompanied our staff on the visit to Aalto's houses.

Nobuyuki Yoshida, Editor in Chief

編集後記

本誌を担当することとなり、遅ればせながらアアルトの作品をこの目で見るべく初めてフィンランドを訪れる機会を得た。もうじき着陸という時、機上から目に飛び込んできたのは森と湖に覆われた大地だった。その時、それまで写真で親しんでいたアアルトの花瓶やランプ、階段など建物を構成するディテールが脳裏に浮かび、この大地がアアルトの建築の原形なのだろうと感じた。

滞在中、今回掲載したアアルト作品他何件か実際に訪問することができ、通俗的な言葉であるが、素直にその空間の質に感動し、心地よさを楽しむことができた。この居心地の良さはいったい何なのだろう？ そして、どうしたらこの空間を誌面で伝えることができるだろうか？ その答えを模索しながら本誌を編集してきた。建物の素材やスケール、物理的な部材の構成など紹介することがその手助けになるのではないかと考え、できるかぎり各作品の詳細図をアアルト財団より提供して頂いた。その何点かの図面には人物や植物も描かれていて、掲載にあたり建築家の姿勢をより表現するべくオリジナルから複写することとした。歳月を経た鉛筆書きからの再現は必ずしも線がクリアに印刷されてはいないが、その点ご理解頂けると幸いである。

この臨時増刊号は、写真家のヤリ・イエッツオネン氏、アアルト美術館のマルック・ラティ氏のご協力なしでは刊行できなかったといっても過言ではない。また、膨大な図面の複写を協力頂いた財団のミーア・ヒッペリ氏、訪問中親切にお世話くださった建築家のサナクセンアホ夫妻、シルッカリーサ・イエッツオネン氏、ハンニ・シッポ氏、新しく配置図を書き起こしてくれたヘランダー／レイヴィスカ事務所の高橋正明氏、他田中雅美氏、林寛治氏等のご協力に深く感謝する次第である。

最後に、消費社会に流されず歴史的な建築物と自然を美しく保全しているフィンランドの人々と文化に改めて敬意を表したいと思う。

(M.A.)

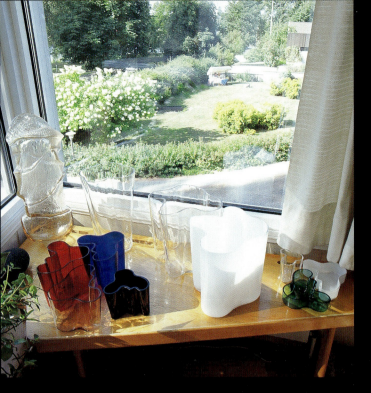

Vases designed by Aalto, in a corner of living room. Villa Skeppet.

シルソ邸の居間にあるアアルトがデザインした花瓶。